THE HEALTHCARE SOLUTION

A STRATEGIC SOLUTION FOR THE
HEALTHCARE REVOLUTION:

STATE HEALTHCARE COOPERATIVES

WAYNE B. ANTHONY
M.Div., M.B.A., CEAP, SPHR

Book Publishers Network
P.O. Box 2256
Bothell • WA • 98041
Pₕ•425-483-3040

10 9 8 7 6 5

Printed in the United States of America

LCCN: 20055923568
ISBN: 1-887542-24-8

Editor: Vicki McCown
Cover: Laura Zugzda
Interior Design and Layout: Stephanie Martindale

Contents

The Healthcare Revolution

The solution for many of America's healthcare challenges is the formation of community or state healthcare cooperatives. In a cooperative an entire community or state could pool its healthcare dollars into a healthcare trust fund. Trustees of the fund could contract with local and regional providers directly or through insurance carriers to provide services for all of their members and dependents at reasonable rates. Patients could choose which provider and services they want, and providers would be paid promptly. Such a structure already exists—ALMOST!

The structure being recommended is a community or state Voluntary Employee Beneficiary Association (VEBA). VEBAs were established in the Employee Retirement Income Security Act of 1974 (ERISA). Over the years, it has been refined by various IRS regulations and tax reform acts. Thus, it is a tried and tested body of legislation and regulation. Moreover, it has broad acceptance from both political parties, business and labor organizations, government agencies and professional entities.

Congress needs to provide three clarifications: first, allow **anyone** in the same geographical area to join rather than limiting it to employees "engaged in the same line of business"; second, allow Healthcare Savings Accounts (HSA) that roll over annually and are portable; third, clarify the use of funds for non-taxable wellness, sickness, and accident benefits when provided by qualified 501(C)(3) healthcare organizations.

All of these clarifications fall within the original intent of the congressional legislation, which was to allow employees from 10 or more small employers to collectively form a healthcare trust in order to purchase healthcare on a broader risk-sharing basis. Because of the restriction embodied in the phrase "same line of business," small businesses have been unable to utilize such a healthcare trust. Instead, VEBAs have been used extensively and successfully by large and mid-sized employers.

A cooperative would make it possible for **anyone** in the same geographical area to participate in a collective healthcare trust and to purchase healthcare services, including wellness, sickness, and accident benefits. A cooperative will benefit everyone, especially those who cannot access large group discounts or who are not covered at all. The cooperative has the added advantage of putting participants in the position of designing the benefit plan, while at the same time having fiduciary responsibility for the financial solvency and stability of the trust. Moreover, it gives participants more <u>choices</u> regarding healthcare providers and health services.

Providers benefit because plan designs and reimbursement are actually directed by the people who pay for and use the services. It puts **purchasers, participants,** and **providers** of healthcare back in charge of healthcare and its delivery system. Equally important, the cooperative encourages, reimburses and rewards wellness, prevention and healthy life styles.

A cooperative arrangement could dramatically improve the way healthcare is delivered, simplify how it is paid, and include everyone in accessible, affordable healthcare coverage. Indeed, what is proposed is a simple but significant amendment to the Trust guidelines that would facilitate the design and intent of the original legislation. Obviously, a community or state healthcare cooperative could have a very positive impact on healthcare for employers, employees, families, unions, physicians, hospitals, clinicians—indeed all purchasers, participants, and providers of healthcare in this country. It could well be the most significant healthcare legislation enacted in years and be the most positive healthcare reform introduced in Congress in decades.

A Tribute to

&

The Contributors

A very special thanks to the following people for the invaluable insights and recommendations they contributed to this book and its proposal:

Mr. Peter Adams, Vice President
    Human Resources Support AFLAC

Mr. Michael Aitken, Director of Governmental Affairs
    Society for Human Resource Management (SHRM)

Ms. Jan Anderson, Professional Counselor
    The Business Resource Center

Ms. Frances Anthony, Professional Counselor
    Columbus Psychological Associates

Mr. Tom Barron, Director, Dept. of Human Resources
    Columbus Consolidated Government

Ms. Alison Bembeck, Legislative Assistant
    Representative John Boehner

Ms. Anne Berryman, Staff Correspondent
    Time Magazine

Hon. Sanford Bishop, Representative, Attorney
     United States Congress

Ms. Clara Brown, Nurse, Administrator, Pine Manor/Oak Manor

Mr. Bo Bryant, Chief of Staff, Representative Mac Collins

Hon. Debbie Buckner, State Representative
     State House of Representatives

Mr. Steve Butler, Chair of the Board, Philanthropist
     W. C. Bradley Co.

Mr. Vergil Cabasco, Legislative Director
     Representative Jennifer Dunn

Mr. Jim Cardin, Human Resources Manager
     Housing Authority of Columbus

Ms. Mary Ann Chaffee, Chief of Staff
     Senator Zell Miller

Hon. Saxby Chambliss, Senator, United States Senate

Mr. Cecil Cheves, Attorney
     Page, Scrantom, Page, Sprouse, Tucker & Ford, PC

Dr. Dean Chipman, Physician

Mr. Mike Collins, Legislative Assistant
     Representative Tom Udall

Hon. Mac Collins, Representative, Business Owner
     United States Congress

Mr. Don Cooper, Chief Human Resources Officer
     Muscogee County School District

Dr. James Crosse, Physician

Mr. Roy Cureton, Senior Director, Corporate Human
     Resource Services, Swift Denim

Dr. Deborah Daniels, Physician

Mr. Dan Danner, Senior Vice President
    National Federation of Independent Business

Mr. Don Dempsey, Legislative Assistant, Senator Jon Kyl

Dr. Bhushit Dixit, Physician

Mr. Watson Donald, III, Legislative Correspondent
    Senator Jeff Sessions

Dr. Thomas Driver, Professor, United States Navy

Mr. Lance Duke, President & CEO, The Medical Center

Ms. Jessica Efrid, Legislative Assistant
    Senator Lindsey Graham

Dr. Jerry Fleischer, Psychologist
    Columbus Psychological Associates

Ms. Tina Flora, Benefits Administrator, Swift Denim

Mr. Shawn Friesen, Legislative Assistant
    Representative Mac Collins

Mr. Archie Galloway, Legislative Assistant
    Senator Jeff Sessions

Mr. George Ganty, Legislative Assistant
    Representative John Boehner

Mr. David Garets, Executive Vice President, Healthlink

Mr. Mike Garrigan, President, CEO, St. Francis Hospital

Mr. Joe Gay, Manager, Human Resources
    Precision Components International

Ms. Raissa Geary, Staff Director, Senator Mike Enzi

Dr. Clark Gillett, Physician

Ms. Elaine Gillispie, Field Representative
Representative Sanford Bishop, Jr.

Mr. Cameron Gilreath, Legislative Assistant
Representative Judy Biggert

Hon. Phil Gingrey, Representative, Physician
United States Congress

Mr. Howard Gleckman, Senior Correspondent
Business Week

Ms. Jane Grace, Legislative Director, Senator Jon Kyl

Ms. Patty Groff, Benefits Accounting Manager
Synovus Financial Corp.

Ms. Becca Hardin, Vice President of Economic Development, Greater Columbus Chamber of Commerce

Mr. Mike Hill, CEO, Evergreen Health Plan, Inc.

Mr. Matt Hoskins, Senior Legislative Assistant
Representative Jim DeMint

Mr. Ed Howard, Healthcare Policy Analyst
Alliance for Health Reform

Dr. Ron Hudson, Physician

Dr. Tommy Hudson, Vice President
Quality Healthcare Partnership, Inc.

Ms. Mary Huttlinger, Manager, Benefits Legislation
Society for Human Resource Management (SHRM)

Ms. Paige Jennings, Legislative Correspondent
Senator John Breaux

Mr. Mike Johnson, Manager of Employment Services, AFLAC

Mr. Wayne Joiner, Vice President, Human Resources
Columbus Regional Healthcare Systems, Inc.

Ms. Debbie Lane, Vice President, Human Resources
Blue Cross/ Blue Shield

Ms. Rena Lane, Benefits Manager & Plan Administrator
AFLAC

Ms. Shari Lewack, Manager, Employee Benefits
Precision Components International

Ms. Caroline Lynch, Legislative Assistant
Representative John Shadegg

Mr. Tom Markson, Healthcare Consultant
Claire House Community

Mr. John McCann, Mental Health Clinician
Columbus Psychological Associates

Mr. Norman McCullough, CEO, Columbus Clinic, P.C.

Mr. Michael Meeks, Vice President, Human Resources
St. Francis Hospital

Hon. Zell Miller, Senator, United States Senate

Mr. Allen Moore, Legislative Director, Senator Bill Frist

Ms. Donna Morgan, Director, Patient Care Services
Columbus Hospice, Inc.

Ms. Deborah Newman, Benefits & Personnel Manager
W. C. Bradley Co.

Ms. Marci Nielson, Department of Legislation, AFL-CIO

Ms. Laura O'Neill, Legislative Assistant
Senator Jeff Sessions

Ms. Millie Paradiso, Human Resources, St. Francis Hospital

Mr. Brent Perry, Legislative Assistant, Senator George Allen

Ms. Anne Phelps, Health Policy Advisor, The White House

Hon. Evelyn Pugh, City Councilor
Columbus Consolidated Government

Ms. Laura Quattlebaum, Legislative Director
Representative Jack Kingston

Mr. Jim Railey, CEO, Quality Healthcare Partnership, Inc.

Ms. Carol Ridley, Director of Risk Management
Synovus Financial Corp.

Ms. Kathy Robbins, Senior Human Resources Analyst
AFLAC

Hon. Mike Rogers, Representative, United States Congress

Mr. Colin Roskey, Legislative Assistant
Senate Finance Committee

Dr. Jack Ross, Physician

Dr. William Roundtree, Physician

Mr. Larry Sanders, President & CEO
Columbus Regional Healthcare Systems, Inc.

Ms. Birgitte Santaella, Senior Staff Assistant
Representative John Shadegg

Ms. Marissa Scalia, Healthcare Policy Analyst
Emory University

Mr. Martin Schey, Attorney, Schey Law Office

Ms. Patricia Schoeni, Executive Director
National Coalition on Health Care

Mr. Rick Service, Managing Director, *Business & Health*

Hon. Jeff Session, Senator, United States Senate

Hon. Richard Shelby, Senator, United States Senate

Mr. Mike Smajd, Executive Director, Columbus Hospice

Dr. David Smith, Physician, St. Francis Hospital

Mr. Brett Smith, Senior Legislative Assistant
  Representative Phil Gingrey

Ms. Mary Stranger, Director of Benefits
  Synovus Financial Corp.

Mr. Doug Stross, Legislative Director
  Representative John Shadegg

Ms. Kay Sullivan, Senior Vice President
  U.S. Chamber of Commerce

Mr. Joseph Summers, Legislative Assistant
  Senator Richard Shelby

Ms. Judy Talley, Operations Coordinator
  The Business Resource Center

Ms. Kathryn Teaster, Senior Healthcare Consultant

Mr. Tyler Thompson, Legislative Correspondent
  Senator Zell Miller

Mr. Neil Trautwein, Director of Employment and Policy
  National Association of Manufacturers

Mr. Bill Turner

Dr. David Varner, Physician

Dr. Tom Wade, Physician

Mr. Hugh Wilson, President/CEO, Doctors Hospital

Mr. Steven Wojcik, Director, Public Policy
  National Business Group on Health

Mr. Rick Woodham, Vice President, Human Resources
  W. C. Bradley Co.

☙

HEALTHCARE IN TRANSITION

In 1900, most healthcare was provided in the home. Doctors made house calls. Hospitals were small, with little medical equipment and mostly regular beds for sick people and nursing care. Specialty hospitals in big cities were often called sanitariums for long-term treatment. Most physicians were general practitioners paid with in-kind gifts, such as food, clothing, furniture, transportation, and office space. Specialists were rare, located at medical schools, and most of them were paid faculty salaries.

In manufacturing communities, the company (employer) provided a job for the employee. Often the employer provided the employee with a house, utilities, transportation, social services, a general store, and a company clinic. Employers helped fund local schools and churches. On the big farm, the owner provided the sharecropper with a house, utilities, food, water, transportation, recreation, and medical care.

Today, almost everything has changed. For the most part, the paternalistic attitudes of the past are gone. Most employers no longer provide employees with general stores, clinics, clothes, houses, utilities, transportation, schools, churches, theaters, vacation spots, lakes, or pools. By and large, most employers pay their employees wages and let them buy their own houses, cars, clothes, utilities, vacation homes, boats, and trips. Most employers give their employees the money and let them choose how to spend it. Employers let their employees choose the goods and services on which they wish to spend their money. Even employers now give their employees money for retirement and let them choose how to invest it.

With one major prevailing exception, employees can choose how they will direct their money (their benefits). The one exception is healthcare.

Today, employers, as well as the government, still take a very *parental* role in choosing for their employees (recipients) and their employees' dependents how their healthcare dollar will be directed (spent). Business and government still "own" most of the allocated healthcare dollars. They direct, through third-party payors, the providers to whom patients may go, how much service they can receive, how much will be paid, by whom it will be paid, and even when it will be paid.

Our current healthcare delivery system is *payor-controlled* and *plan-driven*. Plans designed by the government, the company or the insurance company decide who qualifies for treatment, what treatment is allowed, how much care a person may receive, what it will cost and who will pay, how long they must wait, what conditions must be met, and what is disqualified.

Payors (third-party administrators/insurance plan managers) control the plans, the participants, the patients, and the providers. The task of a plan manager is to manage the plans. The plan design dictates the healthcare. Together they are unaffectionately known as "Managed Care"…they manage healthcare.

For at least twenty-one (21) compelling reasons, we are being propelled into a healthcare transition. Some of the reasons relate to frustrations with the payor-controlled system. Some of the reasons relate to changing demographics and population issues. Some of the reasons relate to medical technology and global epidemiology. Some of the reasons relate to lifestyle choices and healthcare resources. Some of the reasons relate to consumer choice and stakeholder involvement. Some of the reasons relate to healthcare cycles and delivery systems.

More specifically the issues pushing our country into this transition are:

1. The massive frustration with managed care
2. The negative impact of the Patient's Bill of Rights
3. The legal and financial implication of REPAIR
4. The accelerating costs of healthcare
5. The implications of new technology
6. The worldwide availability of medical information
7. The gaping disparitics in mcdical carc
8. The growing demands of the medical consumer
9. The medical and financial implications of an aging population
10. The long-term impact from the neglected generation
11. The massive social and medical threat of global travel
12. The growing problem caused by medical mutations
13. The medical and financial impact of poor lifestyle choices
14. The financial and social implications of over-capitalization
15. The ultimate bankruptcy of an illness treatment delivery system
16. The turf wars and power plays of the medical-industrial complex
17. The long-term ramifications of biogenetic engineering

18. The far-reaching implications of the immortality illusion
19. The bizarre world where healthcare is an entitlement
20. The monumental chaos from population overload
21. The social reprisals of ignoring global warnings

Indeed, we are at the end of a normal phase in the healthcare cycle, which usually occurs every thirty years. What we will transition into is somewhat obvious yet very complex, convincingly clear and yet highly controversial, basically necessary yet very difficult, globally essential and yet personally excruciating.

The fundamental question is "Can we do it wisely?"

The question being asked in decision circles among informed stakeholders is "Can we transition into *patient choice*?" Can we transition into a *participant-directed, participant-directed* healthcare system and do it wisely? Various phrases have been used to refer to this new healthcare delivery system such as:

> Consumer-Choice Healthcare Plans
> Consumer-Designed Healthcare Plans
> Consumer-Directed Healthcare Plans
> Participant-Directed Healthcare Plans
> Patient-Controlled Healthcare Plans
> Defined-Contribution Healthcare Plans

They all relate to a healthcare delivery system that is no longer payor controlled (i.e., managed care controlled), but to a system where the patient (participant) has far more control over his/her healthcare options and choices.

To be sure, these are but some of the forces that are pushing us, kicking and screaming, whining and complaining, into this transition from a payor-controlled healthcare system into a participant-controlled healthcare system; from a plan-designed/

payor-controlled healthcare system to a participant-designed/
participant-controlled healthcare system. Can we, dare we, let
participants make the choices? Can we, dare we, let them live
or die with their decisions?

PART ONE

THE FORCES BEHIND THE REVOLUTION

CHAPTER ONE

A NATIONAL OUTRAGE

The first force about to change the way healthcare is delivered in this country is the growing national outrage with managed care. The political and legal backlash has begun.

Peter Smith met Karin Knudsen at the University of Wisconsin in 1984. They were married in September 1989 and built their first home in 1990.

Karin was bright, athletic, quick-witted, and very health-conscious. She ate a healthy diet, played volleyball, and often jogged ten miles most days. She was an accountant by profession and a member of an HMO. At twenty-four, she noticed vaginal bleeding. The results from the pap smear said she was fine—"normal." The occasional bleeding continued. Another pap smear was submitted, and it too came back "normal." Ten months later another pap smear came back "normal." She was treated for "micro glandular hyperplasia" and was told she had nothing to worry about.

In June of 1990, she passed out after a volleyball game. She had been bleeding continuously for twenty-one days. After an exam, her doctor noted an irritated cervix but told her, "Don't worry. I've seen cancer, and this isn't cancer."

After years of bleeding, three pap smears and three biopsies, Karen Smith finally lost faith in her healthcare plan. She went to a highly regarded gynecologist not affiliated with her HMO and paid his fees out of her own pocket. A gynecological oncologist was consulted. The results were unquestionable: cancer.

The cervical cancer was very advanced. It had by then penetrated her cervix and entered the lymph nodes. From there it had spread throughout her body. Karin, who longed to have children, was immediately scheduled for a radical hysterectomy and chemotherapy. It was to no avail. On March 8th, at the age of twenty-nine, Karin Smith left Peter forever. She had "died of a disease that shouldn't kill any woman receiving routine gynecological care," writes Jan DeBlieu of *Health Magazine* (*Reader's Digest*, July 1997, p.108).

One month before her death, Karin was invited to speak before Congress. She blamed her doctors, and even more, a managed-care system that encouraged speed and impersonal treatment for condemning her to death. "Due to their gross incompetence and shameful errors, I am now dying," she testified.

The companies involved agreed, offering a $6.3 million malpractice settlement. However, Milwaukee County District Attorney Michael McCann was not satisfied. He took the case to a whole new level, bringing *criminal* charges of reckless homicide against those involved. The jury agreed! Suddenly there is a new message here: "Now, when a healthcare provider cuts corners to save money and a patient dies, it's no longer a matter of malpractice. It could be homicide."

❧

CHAPTER TWO

THE PATIENT'S BILL OF RIGHTS

The second force changing the delivery of healthcare is The Patient's Bill of Rights. Compelled and propelled by countless stories like that of Karin Smith, Congress was, by September 2001, at the point of passing a bill to protect patients' rights.

In 1998 at least ten candidates were elected to Congress on the platform of HMO reform. They were elected on the promise that they would do something about "managed care." They joined others like Senator Ted Kennedy and Congressman Charles Norwood, already very actively engaged in legislation to give patients more rights in their healthcare plans and give them the right to sue for damages.

Nearly a dozen bills were introduced and four made it to the floor for a vote:

1. The Patient's Bill of Rights Act of 1999 (S.6/ H.R.358)
2. The Managed Care Reform Act (H.R.719)
3. Promoting Responsible Managed Care Act of 1999 (S.374)
4. Access to Quality Care Act (H.R.216)

On July 15, 1999, the Senate passed S.1344, "The Patient's Bill of Rights," by a vote of fifty-three to forty-seven. It contained provisions to include access to emergency rooms, cancer trials, specialists, obstetricians, and gynecologists while barring gag rules on physicians. It provided for internal and external appeals plus disclosures to patients, but no liability provisions.

Over the objection of House leadership, the House passed H.R.2990 on October 7, 1999, by a vote of 275 to 151. Covering 161 million Americans, the bill established liability when care was denied and gave patients the right to sue their health plan for damages. That meant that not only managed care organizations but the purchasing organizations (employers) that agreed to the design of the health plan and contracted for the services would have been liable. Moreover, patients could have brought suit before a State court jury for compensatory and punitive damages. It also guaranteed access to emergency care, specialists, clinical trials, and choice of doctor. The following is a comparison of both bills.

COMPARING THE CHAMBERS' MANAGED CARE PLANS

The House passed a managed care bill (HR 2723) that would give patients the right to sue their health plans in state courts. The measure was folded into a health tax-and-access bill, and the combined bill moved as HR 2990 to a contentious conference with the Senate, which passed a much narrower bill (S 1344) in July. The battle pitted congressional Republican leaders against President Clinton, who supported the House's more wide-ranging bill.

SENATE BILL (S 1344)

Final vote: 53-47, July 15, 1999

Scope: Varies by provision. Sections affecting 48 million patients in state-regulated plans include access to emergency room care; access to cancer clinical trials; a ban on gag rules; and access for women to obstetricians and gynecologists. Provisions affecting 124 million patients in group plans include internal and external appeals. Provisions affecting all 161 million privately insured people include access to breast cancer treatment and tax provisions.

Liability: No provision.

Emergency Care: Guarantees treatment at any emergency room without preauthorization if a "prudent layperson" would deem it necessary, if plan covers emergency care. The plan would not necessarily be forced to cover care outside the emergency department.

Gag Rules: Similar provision to House bill.

Internal Appeals: Requires plans to respond within 30 days to a patient's internal appeal of a denial of coverage, and within

---

HOUSE BILL (HR 2990, INCLUDING HR 2723)

Final vote: 275-141, Oct. 7, 1999

Scope: Covers all 161 million privately insured Americans.

Liability: Allows patients who claim they have been physically or mentally injured when denied care by their health plans to sue in state court for damages. Plans that have complied with external review decisions would not be subject to punitive damages, and any state caps on damages would apply.

Emergency Care: Guarantees treatment at any emergency room without preauthorization if a "prudent layperson" would deem it necessary, if plan covers emergency care.

Gag Rules: Bars plans from restricting what a doctor may tell a patient without treatment options.

Internal Appeals: Requires plans to respond within 14 days, unless an extension is granted, to a patient's internal appeal of a

72 hours in urgent cases. Any patient whose internal review is rejected could appeal to an independent reviewer.

External Appeals: A patient whose internal appeal is rejected could appeal to an independent, external reviewer who must issue a binding, final decision within 72 hours in case of an emergency. Otherwise, the general time limit is approximately 65 days. A patient would be informed within 30 days after that decision is made. If recommended treatment is not provided, patients could obtain it either within the plan or from another provider, and the plan would be liable for the charges and up to $10,000 in fines. To be appealed, one of the requirements would be that the treatment would have to be covered by the plan using its definition of medical necessity. A patient could appeal if he or she is seeking a treatment that might be considered "experimental" in some instances.

Medical Necessity: Independent review boards could consider, but not be bound by, doctor recommendations on medical necessity in handing down decisions.

Woman's Health: Allows women to receive routine gynecological care without a referral from their primary care physician.

Access to Specialists: Requires plans that cover specialty care to allow patients access to specialists "in a timely manner," as determined by medical circumstances.

denial of coverage, and within 72 hours in urgent cases. Any patient whose internal review is rejected could appeal to an external reviewer.

External Appeals: Any patient whose internal appeal is rejected could appeal to an independent, external reviewer who must issue a binding, final decision within 72 hours in case of an emergency, or 21 days otherwise. Penalties could include federal court action, such as civil fines of up to $1,000 per day. Plans that repeatedly violate review decisions could be fined up to $500,000.

Medical Necessity: Guarantees that doctors, not health plan officials, would determine what treatment is medically necessary. Patients could appeal an internal appeal decision that found a treatment medically unnecessary or experimental.

Women's Health: Allows women to receive routine gynecological care without a referral from their primary care physicians.

Access to Specialists: Requires plans that cover specialty care to provide referrals for such care when needed, including treatment by out-of-network providers if no appropriate specialist is available in the network.

Whistleblower Protections: No provision.

Whistleblower Protections: Medical professionals who report any actions by a plan affecting quality of care for patients would be protected. No plan could retaliate against a protected health professional.

Choice of Doctors: Allows workers for companies with 50 employees or more to visit doctors who are not in their plan's network. Plans could charge more for this option.

Choice of Doctors: Permits patients to choose a point-of-service option if their plan does not offer such access to non-network providers. Plans could charge more for this option.

Access to Clinical Trials: Requires plans to cover routine patient costs associated with cancer clinical trials sponsored by the National Institutes of Health, the Department of Defense or Department of Veterans' Affairs.

Access to Clinical Trials: Requires plans to allow certain patients access to clinical trials testing new treatments and cover routine costs of care.

Tax Provisions: Several similar provisions. Does not include HealthMarts and association health plans (AHP).

Tax Provisions: Expands a current pilot program for tax-exempt medical savings accounts. Also allows full deduction of long-term care insurance. The self-employed also would be able to deduct all of the costs of health insurance premiums. Allows groups to pool resources through entities known as HealthMarts or association health plans (AHPs) to buy more affordable insurance.

Both bills were referred to a Joint Senate and House Conference Committee to "work out the differences." During the entire year of 2000, Congress tried to find common ground on the extent of liability. Unfortunately, they could not agree on the liability issues of both bills and a compromise bill never cleared the committee. Both pieces of legislation died with the 106th Congress.

At the beginning of the 107th Congress, Senator John McCain (R-AZ) shocked the country when he joined forces with Ted Kennedy (D-MA) and John Edwards (D-NC) to introduce S. 283. The Bipartisan Patient Protection Act of 2001 was very similar to the previous "Patient's Bill of Rights." According to the Society for Human Resource Management (SHRM) Legislative Fact Sheet (March, 2001), S. 283 allowed lawsuits against managed care firms and employers in both state and federal courts. These lawsuits could have been filed before an independent review of a denied claim was complete. It not only allowed for recovery of economic damages (medical expenses and lost wages), but also permitted lawsuits for compensatory damages (pain and suffering) and punitive damages (punishment of the company) for up to $5 million. Attorneys could get up to 50 percent of the award and class-action lawsuits would be allowed. The bill would have made corporate officers personally liable.

On Friday evening, June 29, 2001, the Senate passed the Kennedy/McCain/ Edwards patient bill of rights legislation by a vote of 59 to 36. The Bipartisan Patient Protection Act of 2001 (S. 283) was the first major legislation passed by the then Democratic-controlled Senate and reflected the work of the Health, Education, Labor, and Pension Committee then chaired by Senator Edward Kennedy (*H.R. Voice*, July 6, 2001).

On Thursday evening, August 2, 2001, the House passed by a party line vote of 218 to 213 the Norwood/Bush compromise bill. Introduced by Charles Norwood (R-GA) in consultation with President Bush, the bill allowed patients the right to sue for all damages in both state and federal court. However, it limited the awards to $1.5 million if the plan ignored an appeal board's decision. The bill also included access to all emergency rooms and a choice of doctors. Basically, independent review boards could override legitimate, legal, contractual arrangements, provisions, and designs of healthcare plans. And every state could have different standards (*H.R. Voice*, August 3, 2001).

Congress went into August recess with both bills again referred to a Senate-House Conference Committee. Because of the attack on America on September 11, 2001, the subsequent War on Terrorism, and the war in Iraq, the Conference Committee never met. However, healthcare has become a national issue again because of the dramatic increases in healthcare premiums.

CHAPTER THREE

R.E.P.A.I.R.

The third force changing the delivery of healthcare is Richard F. Scruggs and the so-called REPAIR team. According to *H.R. News* (June, 2000, p.33), "REPAIR" is an acronym for RICO and ERISA Prosecutors Advocating for Insurance Industry Reform. The team of prosecutors from across the country has been organized and partially funded by Dickie Scruggs.

Dickie Scruggs is a trial lawyer from Pascatoula, Mississippi, who took on the asbestos industry in the 1970s and won a class-action suit. Then he took on the tobacco industry. With the help of dozens of law firms and attorney generals from across the country, he launched a class-action suit against big tobacco and won a $150 *billion* judgment!

Using the nearly $1 billion he was paid, he has created a "war chest" to take on his next big target—HMOs. He targeted the country's five largest HMOs, claiming they are guilty of consumer fraud, racketeering, extortion, and medical malpractice. According to a *60 Minutes* report (February 29, 2000), he filed massive class-action lawsuits on behalf of the 32 million people represented by United Health, Cigna, PacifiCare, Humana, and Aetna.

These companies represent the first wave of defendants. In fact, all HMOs, health insurance companies, third-party administrators, and even self-funded plans could eventually be included. According to the lawsuits, any third-party payor that sells health coverage with the "promise to deliver quality healthcare" and then limits services, creates artificial barriers, complicates the process, or causes people to "jump through all sorts of hoops before they pay the bill" is guilty of *consumer fraud* and *racketeering*.

In addition, any healthcare organization that contracts with licensed medical personnel, that is "puts doctors on their payroll and then tells the doctors what they can and cannot treat," is practicing medicine without a license. Moreover, these organizations have "corrupted the practice of medicine by using financial incentives to force doctors to under-treat their patients" and they may be liable for *negligence, malpractice,* and *reckless homicide.*

It is no wonder that "Dickie Scruggs is also working Washington, D.C., pushing for a Patient's Bill of Rights," said *60 Minutes* reporters. The proposed bill spelled out what HMO customers could expect: the right to a second opinion, the right to see a specialist, and *the right to sue.*" While it contained that provision granting the right to sue, the question was who in the chain of decision-making will be held liable?

With Dickie Scruggs and his well-funded "armada of law firms" going after the managed care industry on behalf of 30 to 80 million people with jury trials, seeking multibillion-dollar compensatory and punitive damages, a massive change began to occur in the healthcare delivery system. Healthcare payors (HMOs, insurance companies, self-funded plans, and TPAs) have become increasingly reluctant to deny any claim, preauthorization (precertification), or request for services. Healthcare purchasers (employers) may become more reluctant to limit any healthcare service in their plan design and summary plan descriptions. As a result, healthcare costs are rising at nearly 20 percent annually.

CHAPTER FOUR

ACCELERATING COSTS

A fourth force changing healthcare is the accelerating rise in healthcare costs. Fifteen percent of today's payroll is deducted to pay for social security and Medicare (FICA). According to the Social Security Administration (Goodman, p.56), in the year 2050, it will rise to 55 percent. Today's employees pay an average of $3,055 per year. By 2025, that amount will be $6,000 (Goodman, p.44). From 1990 to 1999, medical inflation averaged 6 percent. In the year 2000, it accelerated to 9 percent, in 2001 it rose to 11 percent, and in 2002 it went up to 14 percent.

According to the Health Care Financing Administration (Miller, p.337), Americans spent only 3.5 percent of the Gross Domestic Product (GDP) in 1929 on medical care. By 1940, it had risen to 4.0 percent; by 1950 to 4.5 percent; by 1960 to 5.3 percent; by 1970 to 7.6 percent; by 1980 to 10 percent; by 1993 to 14 percent; and if the trend continues, by 2025 it will be 33 percent; by 2050 it will be 75 percent; and by 2062, we will spend 100 percent of everything we make to treat our illnesses (Goodman, p.15; Castro, p.28). That is unless something significant is done.

Eugene Steurele (Goodman, p.78) added all of the direct expenses paid for healthcare (insurance premiums, employee contributions, out-of-pocket expenses, co-pays) plus indirect expenses (payroll taxes, reduced wages, the employer-provided portions, and contributions) and computed that "illness care" costs the average household over $8,000 per year or 19.4 percent of their income.

Janet Castro, Health Editor for *Time* magazine (Castro, p.28), reminds us that in 1963, America spent only 6 percent of its GDP on health services. By 1993 that amount had escalated to 14 percent, one and one half times any other industrialized nation in the world! She predicts that "without substantial intervention in the way the system works," the United States will be spending 33 percent of its resources in 2025 and 75 percent of all its resources by the year 2050 on medicine.

Castro reveals some other shocking statistics. One percent of the population generated 29 percent of medical expenses. Five percent of the population creates 50 percent of all medical expenses. One-third of all healthcare expenses occur in the last six months of life, and as much as 35 percent of all Medicare expenses may be knowingly "futile procedures." Doctors and family know the additional medical expenditures will only sustain a near vegetative form of life for a matter of hours or, at most, a few days.

Every year, $100 billion dollars is spent on "unnecessary procedures"; $200 billion is spent on "defensive medicine"; $100 billion is spent on paperwork alone; $13 billion consists of unpaid bills; $22 billion is shifted to private-pay patients; and $75 billion results from theft and fraud. In 1992 alone, the Fortune 500 companies suffered $69.5 billion in losses because of unbudgeted healthcare costs. The projected tab for retiree benefits alone now exceeds $1 trillion.

Medical inflation soared in the 1970s and 1980s to as high as 18 percent per year. Managed care brought it back to less than 5 percent per year during the 1990s. However, premiums and expenses are already on the rise: 12 percent to 100 percent increases have been reported by large companies. Nationwide healthcare costs are rising nearly 20 percent annually. Because of rising costs, a major healthcare crisis is near. For some individuals and organizations, it is already here.

CHAPTER FIVE

❧

TECHNOLOGY

A fifth force creating a crisis in the American healthcare system is medical technology. The science of medicine has become highly technical, highly expansive, and highly expensive.

Dr. Elliott Rosenberg wrote the following letter to the Editor of *The New York Times* on September 19, 1991, (Goodman, p. VIII) about the case of an eighty-year-old man who was "slowing down." Despite his physician's counsel that this was perfectly normal at age eighty, the man and his wife went on "a medical shopping spree." The physician explained:

> "A few days ago the couple came in for a follow-up visit. They were upset. At their daughter's insistence, they had gone to an out-of-town neurologist. She had wanted the 'best' for her father and would spare no (Medicare) expense to get it. The patient had undergone a CAT scan, an MRI, a spinal tap, a brain stem evoke potential, and a carotid duplex ultrasound. No remediable problems were discovered…
>
> "Instead, the couple was 'emotionally exhausted' and 'anxious' over their co-pays and very upset. Meanwhile, they had run up multi-thousand dollar medical bills that the working taxpayer must pay. All

19

of this because he was naturally aging and his daughter wanted the 'best' medical care *someone else's money* could buy."

As Goodman and Musgrove (p. VIII) put it: "The potential demand for healthcare is virtually unlimited. Even if there were a limit to what medical science can do (which, over time, there isn't), there is almost an endless list of ailments that can motivate our desire to spend. About 83 million people suffer from insomnia, 70 million have severe headaches, 32 million have arthritis, 23 million have allergies, and 16 million have bad backs."

The average cost for these ailments are:

Hip Replacement	$20,000
Heart Transplant	$100,000
Sleep Assessment	$10,000
Kidney Transplant	$100,000
Back Surgery	$15,000
Liver Transplant	$150,000
Heart Surgery	$30,000
Bone Marrow Transplant	$150,000
MRI Scan	$2,500
Premature Babies	$100,000
Cancer Treatment	$30,000
Nursing Home (per year)	$ 36,000
CAT Scan	$2,000

Goodman and Musgrove continue, "There is no limit to what can be repaired or replaced. The only question is how many, how much, how often, how long, and who will pay."

Janet Castro (p.30) related a case with similar options (expensive surgery), but with a different decision by a loving daughter:

"My mother was dying of cancer," recalls one Californian, "and they wanted to take off her leg. She asked me what I thought. I told her to go home and be with Dad! She didn't have much time."

Perhaps one of the most loving gifts a family can give to each other is to love them into life, love them through life, and love them beyond life.

To come into this world means that someday all of us must leave it. One of the wisest, wealthiest, and most powerful humans to have ever lived put it this way: "There is a time to be born and there is a time to die." Perhaps the crisis of healthcare in the twenty-first century will help us learn how to live and learn how to die.

CHAPTER SIX

THE INTERNET

A sixth force already altering the way healthcare is delivered in this country and around the world is the Internet. Newspapers, then magazines, then radio, then television, and then video brought medical information directly to the patient or relative. However, nothing can compare with the Internet for providing the patient, family, and friends and colleagues with massive amounts of medical information.

With the click of a word search, people all over the world have access to volumes of healthcare material. This information is instantaneous, extensive, overwhelming, often state-of-the-art, can be misleading and inaccurate, and is usually free.

With a few more clicks, one can hyperlink to supporting materials, research results, providers, resources, procedures, pharmaceuticals, treatment protocols, pictures, diagnostic data and treatment guidelines.

With a few more clicks, this material can be downloaded to one's own hard drive or printed on paper. The material can be e-mailed to family and friends, even to one's primary care physician or specialist.

Once upon a time, physicians and specialists knew more than their patients about healthcare. They knew more than *anyone* in the community. They were the expert! They knew state-of-the-art medicine and enough about the profession to be *the* primary authority. Medical books and materials were somewhat available to the public, but who knew where to go or took the time to do the research? Doctors were the experts. No one questioned their knowledge or authority.

Now the Internet is turning the world of medicine upside down. Patients, relatives, and lawyers have instant access to more information about medicine than physicians can ever store in their heads. Patients have instant access to more of the latest research, data, diagnoses, pictures, procedures, protocols, outcomes, providers, and prognoses than physicians can possibly assimilate. The Internet is dramatically changing the way physicians (in fact, all providers) practice medicine.

Patients now report going to their physicians and being asked what they, the patients, think is wrong, why they think so, what they know about the problem, and even what they think needs to be done about it. The patient is being asked to give a diagnosis and treatment plan!

Physicians report that patients are now coming to them with printouts of medical information related to their problem along with medical advice on treatment protocols. Many physicians are not only tolerating but also welcoming this wave of *informed* patients. They are incorporating this new medical information into their own analysis and recommendations. They are also recording the patients' comments and making copies of the material for the patients' medical files. This is especially true if the physician disagrees in any way with the diagnosis or treatment protocol.

The Internet will change the way medical care is delivered. As patients and relatives become more confident with the information they receive, they will go less and less to their primary care providers for confirmation. As more products can be ordered over the Internet or over the counter, physician referral will be required less and less. And as primary care providers gain access directly, or through their patients to medical information, consultation with specialists may actually decline.

The Internet is already changing how, when, and where medical procedures are being done. Through the Internet, specialists can now perform surgery on someone hundreds, even thousands of miles away. Medical specialists at major teaching institutions, such as at the Medical College of Georgia, are now linked to specially equipped operating rooms in rural Georgia. Surgeons looking through cameras and operating electronic, robotic arms can perform surgery long distance.

Before the twenty-first century passes, highly skilled medical care will "go" to remote towns, villages, and communities around the world. Floating hospitals, mobile clinics, airborne emergency rooms, and rail-borne medical complexes staffed by medical technicians can take the state-of-the-art to every corner of the world. Specialists concentrated in high-tech teaching centers can deliver advanced medicine around the globe electronically.

The implications are enormous!

One significant implication is the location and number of specialists needed. Currently, specialists are connected to fixed, high-tech facilities—hospitals. Delivering advanced medical procedures through the Internet in state-of-the-art mobile facilities may concentrate specialists around very advanced, high-tech teaching hospitals and medical centers. Moreover, it may change staffing patterns and facility needs at physician offices, local hospitals, and military bases.

Another major implication is the nature, location and equipment needs of primary, secondary, and tertiary medical facilities, nationally and globally. Just one hundred years ago, the physician's office in small towns across America usually consisted of a donated room on the first floor of a small office with the living quarters above. The "office" contained a desk, table, cabinet for medicine, bookshelves, ceramic washbasin, and couch or bed. The physician lived above the office and was on call 24 hours a day, 7 days a week.

"Hospitals" were either community or company clinics or sanitariums in major cities. They were managed by a big company or by a local community. Most towns in America were fortunate to have one hospital. In fact, it was the Hill-Burton Act in the 1940s that encouraged and enabled the building of hospitals across America, just sixty years ago.

The earlier hospitals of the twentieth century (1900-1910) may have had an "emergency" or "surgery" room. If so, it usually consisted of a big meat cutter's table, a cabinet for medicine, and table with ceramic or porcelain basins and water pitchers. This was the nature of medical facilities and surgical equipment just one hundred years ago. Hospital rooms consisted of wrought iron or wooden beds, open windows, wooden chairs, and wooden chests of drawers. In most hospitals there was no running water, no electricity, and no air-conditioning. Heat came from a pot-bellied stove, water was drawn from wells or springs, and light came from kerosene lanterns.

The community doctor (usually just one) in the early 1900s lived above the office and was available when anyone had an emergency. Sometimes doctors saw people at the office. However, they usually made house calls on horseback or in a buggy. They carried most of the medical equipment that existed in their "black bag." Prescription drugs consisted of a few balms, a few elixirs, and a bottle of whiskey.

In just one hundred years, the healthcare delivery system has changed dramatically. The sheer cost of keeping up with the exploding world of medical technology, high-tech equipment, bio-technical engineering, biological transplants, mechanical replacements, and sophisticated procedures will drive more local hospitals to become emergency centers and short-term clinics, extended-care facilities, and assisted living facilities. One or two hospitals in a multi-county area will become primary and secondary hospitals for routine surgery, obstetrics, gynecology, pediatrics, ongoing cancer treatments, and basic orthopedics, as well as Internet outpatient follow-up. Only major regional university medical centers will offer residential, sophisticated surgery, intensive care, and Internet surgeons and specialists.

It is mind-boggling to think of how little "medicine" changed from Hippocrates in the fifth century B.C. to 1900 A.D.—twenty-five centuries—and then how much it has changed in less than one century. Imagine what the next one hundred years, even the next twenty years, will bring.

❦

CHAPTER SEVEN

MEDICAL DISPARITY

A seventh force changing the delivery of healthcare is called "medical disparity." Medical disparity occurs at several levels. The first level is *economical*. Poor people in this country, indeed in the world, receive less healthcare. Some limitations occur because of choice, some because of awareness, and some because of circumstances.

Good healthcare is directly correlated to the economic well-being of individuals. Better healthcare is directly connected to the average income of a community. As the average income of the community goes up, the quality and access to good healthcare goes up proportionally. There is a limit, however. As a group, the wealthy are not as healthy as the upper middle class. An affluent lifestyle is not always a healthy lifestyle, and the very wealthy may often postpone routine physicals and preventive medicine.

Location is a major factor in medical disparities. Poor communities and countries have older facilities with older equipment and less experienced staff. Major urban and inner-city hospitals are overburdened, understaffed, overwhelmed, and underfunded. They must deal with more chronic and traumatic cases and have inadequate staff, facilities, and equipment to meet the accelerating demand.

Rural and remote hospitals suffer a similar fate. They too are plagued with more chronic, long-term patients using older, often antiquated, facilities and equipment. The most pressing dilemma for rural and remote areas is access to adequate, well-trained medical personnel. Thus, the second level on disparity is *geographical*.

Alfred and Maria Miller (Health Care Financial Administrative Report, p.255) describe this second disparity as "misdistribution" of medical personnel. The federal and state government tried to remedy this situation in the 1950s with a loan program that could be canceled with up to four years of service for primary care physicians. For every year of service in a rural or inner city area, one year of medical school loans would be paid off by the government.

Today, because the demand for primary care physicians is so great in suburban areas, hospitals and group practices pay off the loans simply to get primary care physicians. Moreover, some young physicians and their families are so anxious to settle into affluent America that they are starting suburban practices and paying off these low-interest loans themselves.

A third disparity is *educational*. This is not simply related to formal education. It also relates, more specifically, to health education and awareness. There is a correlation between education and healthcare. The more academic education a person has, in general, the more informed about healthcare that person becomes. Many have received some formal health education in school—physical education, health, biology, anatomy, physiology, and first aid. Such individuals have a propensity to read more material, including health material. They will more likely watch science and discovery shows including health and medical programs. They will more likely access reference material, Internet resources, and professional sources.

Educated people tend to know more about their benefits and how to access them. They tend to know more about prevention techniques and programs and tend to utilize prevention services and health promotion programs. They tend to respond more quickly to symptoms and seek medical information and advice sooner. In general, more educated people follow healthier lifestyles and live longer. Awareness of, access to, and utilization of healthcare information thus makes a difference in healthcare—promotion, prevention, and treatment.

A fourth disparity is *cultural*. Some people are socialized to avoid healthcare. They are taught that it is "weak," "soft," or "sissy" to seek medical help. They may be taught to mistrust the medical/healthcare system or they may be taught other means of illness care through witch doctors, religious practices, herbal remedies, or ancient procedures. Seeking medical advice or attention is contrary to their upbringing or belief system.

As population densities increase, cultures intermingle, and diseases mutate and multiply. Remaining a cultural or individual island is becoming a more dangerous option. Every member of the global community must take responsibility for the health of one and all.

CHAPTER EIGHT

PATIENT POWER

An eighth force changing healthcare is "patient power." Another name is consumerism. An interview with a recent couple describes the new healthcare consumer:

He owned his own multi-staff, million-dollar business for years. He recently sold his business and retired to slow down. His wife developed cancer. After going to several local physicians, she agreed to surgery and subsequent chemotherapy treatments. Some months after chemotherapy, the cancer reappeared. Local physicians advised additional intense chemotherapy with little or no hope of recovery. "I was told it was useless. I was going to die," she said.

The husband and wife refused to accept the local physician's fatal prognosis. They researched the Internet for the best cancer facility in the country. They concluded the best place to go was M. D. Anderson in Houston, Texas. They contacted the facility themselves. They then asked (and had to demand) that their doctor call the facility for an appointment and send their medical records. From then on, they took control of their own case, went to M. D. Anderson, and received great treatment.

She commented, "I am alive today because I didn't take 'die' for a final answer. I refused to let my doctor have the last word!"

That's the new consumer of healthcare services! This new consumer will transform the way healthcare is directed and delivered. These consumers will no longer simply be told what to do, when they can do it, who will do it—without question. The rule of "M. Dieties" is over.

I use this illustration as opposed to many others because this is a post-sixty-five-year-old couple—senior citizens! They are a part of the World War II generation, the organizational generation and the authority-minded generation. They grew up in the scientific period of medicine from 1950 to 1980 when science of every kind dominated the world landscape and scientists in all fields were respected and revered. This was the golden age of universities and university professors. This was the golden age of rocket scientists, aerospace engineers, civil engineers, mechanical engineers, chemists, mathematicians, computer (mainframe) scientists, and the organizations that supplied and serviced their industries.

It was also a golden age of scientific medicine in which medicine moved from the practice of medicine to the *science* of medicine. Between 1920 and 1950, general practice doctors, local drugstore operators, and registered nurses made the practice of medicine up-close and personal.

The age of science (1950 to 1980) changed the attitude and valuation of the practitioners of medicine. No longer was the care of patients as important as the treatment of illnesses. No longer were the people skills of physicians as important as the scientific skills of physicians. No longer was the knowledge and relationship with the person as important as the knowledge and expertise of medicine. Doctors, nurses, and pharmacists were trained in academic settings to amass massive amounts of medical (scientific) information. Learning medicine in medical schools became brutal marathons for cramming information, knowledge, and science. Those marathons often lasted eight to sixteen years after high school. And when they finished—they had arrived. The smartest and most knowledgeable became specialists. The very brightest and most knowledge-filled became faculty at teaching hospitals and research centers. We made medical scientists out of our medical people and rewarded them according to the amount of scientific education they obtained and the number of degrees they achieved.

As a result, from 1950 to 1980, there was an incredible increase in reimbursement from insurance carriers to specialists. For general practitioners, pediatricians, internists, and family practitioners, where less scientific education was required but more patient care was involved, the reimbursement for their time and expertise remained low and has become embarrassingly disparate.

In the last twenty years, the whole world has challenged the sacredness of science. Ask science and math professors in universities to relate how valued they feel today as compared to business and legal professors. Talk to aerospace engineers, automotive engineers, and even computer engineers about what has happened to their fields, jobs, and pay over the last twenty years.

The world of scientific medicine is being turned upside down as well. The primary care physician has become the gatekeeper to specialists, biotech labs are more attractive than medical schools, and the revenue for complementary medicine and related health products is expanding while the reimbursement for traditional medicine and illness care services is shrinking.

Most of all, the patient has a mind. They want their mind recognized by physicians. Patients have a voice and they want their voice heard. Patients and the relatives want to know the why, when, and what about medical options. They want access, acknowledgment, answers, and more than one option. They want more than one opinion.

Patients and their relatives are seeking and demanding information and answers. They are using the Internet, libraries, self-help books, periodicals, and manufacturers' literature to inform themselves, inform their doctors, challenge their prognosis and protocols, discuss other options, and even propose their own treatment plan.

The word of the doctor is no longer the only word, nor is it the last word. Knowledge is power. Physicians can no longer possess all the knowledge. No longer can they possess all the power. Patients and those related to them are becoming knowledgeable. As a result, they are exerting their power in medical decisions as never before.

The truth is this may turn out to be a good thing for everyone. Physicians and other medical practitioners may come to appreciate all of this extra research assistance. This well-informed patient who is helping make the diagnosis and proposing treatment options will take some of the life-or-death pressure off the physician. The health-minded, unthreatened medical professional can now have a new partner in the decision-making process. When patients have helped make the decision, they have buy-in and are more likely to follow through with treatment and less likely to file suit for malpractice. They helped make the decision!

Patients and related parties who are treated like reasonable people, who are consulted in the process, and who are given the final decision will be more pleased with the process, more comfortable with the procedures, and more content with the outcome. They certainly will not and cannot lay *all* the blame on the medical provider. They can and should take some credit when the plan works. Everyone is part winner; no one is the sole loser.

This, too, begins to rebalance the life and work of a medical provider. It begins to rebalance medical knowledge with patient relationships. It reconnects knowledge, skills, and ability with compassion, care, and relationship. It restores both the *technique* and the *touch* of medicine. It's high-tech and high-touch. It's competency and connectedness. It's the profession of medicine along with the practice of medicine.

It is really why most people went into medicine in the first place—to take care of people, not to perform procedures on living cadavers. This puts them back in real *touch* with real people.

CHAPTER NINE

❧

AN AGING POPULATION

The ninth force that is changing healthcare is an aging population. Our population is getting older and living longer. This older population is getting larger and sicker. Plus, the number of people living past eighty, even one hundred years of age will grow, and the number and percentage of the population over sixty-five will increase through the twenty-first century. Their medical problems, our medical problems, will be multiple, complex, and costly.

Consider some alarming statistics: In 1900 (just one hundred years ago), the average life expectancy was forty-seven; in 2000, the average life expectancy has climbed to seventy-eight! If the aging rate for this century continues, the average life expectancy in 2100 (one hundred years from now) will be 140! If the aging rate since 1950 continues, in 2100 the average life expectancy will be closer to 160 or even 170 years old.

By the year 2010, Baby Boomers (born between 1945 and 1960), which is the largest demographic group, will be over fifty years of age. In fact, in 2010 more people in America will be over fifty than under fifty. By 2010, there will be one person receiving Social Security for every one person funding Social Security!

Centenarians are the fastest growing age group in America, and by the year 2050 the average life expectancy will be one hundred. The cost of providing long-term care is now $60 billion. If the population trends continue and the treatment patterns continue, the annual price tag by 2025 (in just twenty-three years) will exceed $4 trillion.

Medical technology now allows us to replace joints, limbs, hearts, kidneys, lungs, livers, eyes, bone marrow, and blood. Virtually any body part can be replaced, repaired, or bypassed. As one physician said, "We can now virtually rebuild a person." What was science fiction forty years ago is now science reality today and will be common practice tomorrow.

The most compelling and controversial questions for this century are how much care, for whom, and how long? Tied to these questions are what medical procedures will be provided for whom, and at what age?

The first controversial issue is age. At what point will age become a major factor in determining eligibility for medical products and surgical proceedures?

The second issue is money. What will be done, for whom, and who pays: Government or business? Individuals or groups?

The third issue is value. Who will receive what services and for what purpose. Will productivity be a factor? Will the question be "What contribution is that individual making to society and for how much longer?" Does one's ability to continue to contribute to society affect who gets what? Who makes that decision?

The fourth issue is lifestyle. Does one's past lifestyle and previous health choices influence who gets what, when, and how much? If a person has, in the past, or currently participates in high-risk lifestyles, are they given an equal opportunity at a limited supply of medical resources? Does a person's previous history of destructive lifestyles influence the decision? Should a liver transplant go to a heavy-drinking, rich, freewheeling, big-spending former athlete or to a devout, faithful, dedicated, community-minded surgeon? Should a lung transplant go to a seventy-year-old, lifetime heavy smoker or a thirty-year-old, health-conscious, high school P.E. teacher?

The leadership of this planet in this century must face the realities of and deal with healthcare-related decisions that have been ignored or postponed for decades. There is an exploding demand for all medical options possible. There is also an exponential proliferation of medical options conceivable. However, there is a physical restriction on the medical options available. Plus, there is also an economic limitation on the medical options affordable. Thus, there is an unlimited worldwide demand for medical services; however, there is a limited worldwide supply of medical resources.

The incredibly tough decisions that must be faced by the leaders of this century as well as this millennium are mind-boggling and heart-wrenching. Dealing with a rapidly aging population is but one.

CHAPTER TEN

❧

THE NEGLECTED POPULATION

A tenth force already having an alarming impact on global healthcare is the declining investment in children's health. While more and more of the healthcare dollars are being consumed by older people, less and less money is being invested in the care of children. They are the most neglected and least served, most vulnerable and least powerful of all segments of our society and around the world.

Moreover, they suffer a disproportionate amount of dehydration, hunger, malnutrition, starvation, disease, infection, exposure, injuries, cruelty, and inhumanity.

Ironically, in a nation and world of great resources, the disparity is only accelerating. As a nation we spend 80 percent of our healthcare dollars on the *last* eighty days of life. More alarming is the fact that we spend 80 percent of our healthcare dollar on people over sixty-five and only 2 percent on people under eighteen. Factor out premature babies and cancer treatment for children and the amount we spend to keep children healthy and well is only 0.03 percent (3/100 of a percent)—less than one-tenth of 1 percent of our so called healthcare dollars!

Four out of ten children are born to teenagers. Six out of ten of those children were born out of wedlock. Four out of ten children are born into poverty and six out of ten children are being raised by a single parent.

Four alarming results are occurring. Unborn children are receiving inadequate prenatal care, nutrition, and medical care, plus exposure to maternal stress, substance abuse, and violence. An increasing number of premature children are being physically saved by high-risk nurseries. Yet in every conceivable way, they are behind—birth weight, lung and kidney functioning, body development, mental capacity, and emotional health. Their tiny bodies are subjected to weeks and months of pain and suffering. They have limited physical and emotional attachment. They survive physically, but at what price—physically, emotionally, socially, as well as financially? Are our national resources adequately focused on this multi-decade problem?

The lack of focus on children gets worse. Newborn and preschool children are getting less care, food, water, and nutrition than ever before. Today's children get inadequate medical care, inadequate parenting, inadequate or restrictive educational, social, physical, or recreational opportunities. The first five years of life for two out of three children in America is a war zone of violence, neglect, abuse, malnutrition, poverty, and chaos. It is a world of terror! There is little or limited food, water, clothing, housing, medicine, and parental support. Many have no extended family.

Elementary-aged children are receiving less healthy diets, living more sedentary lives, and learning fewer coping skills. More children are overweight and participating in fewer physical activities. Obesity in children is an alarming trend.

Fourteen percent of America's children are medically obese, yet they live in a world where 40 percent of the world's children are starving. According to an ABC Report (02-13-02) the actual percentage of child obesity is higher—25 percent (one out of four). Moreover, 70 percent of the children in the world are suffering some degree of malnutrition, and we have an epidemic of obesity!

More children today lack healthy adult relationships and positive role models than ever before. Often they see poor eating, sleeping, and drinking habits, as well as poor working, coping, and relating skills. Many children are living in environments with substance abuse, sexual abuse, criminal conduct, antisocial behavior, educational underachievers, and vocational apathy. We may well be producing cultural problems of epic proportion for generations to come.

America's healthcare expenditures must become more balanced. More of our healthcare and human service dollars must be invested in programs and services that support children and their caregivers.

1. Responsible parenting
2. Prenatal care
3. Parental support
4. Newborn services
5. Child care
6. Immunizations
7. After-school activities
8. Child protection
9. Child advocacy
10. Health promotion
11. Wellness promotion
12. Nutrition
13. Exercise
14. Sports involvement
15. Music lessons
16. Recreational opportunities
17. Body image awareness
18. Family survival
19. Self-esteem

20. Wholeness promotion
21. Success building
22. Community involvement
23. Vocational training
24. Education success
25. Social skills

Unless America rethinks and reprograms its healthcare and human service dollars toward children and their health and well-being, then we will grow an increasingly unhealthy society—not just physically but emotionally, morally, and socially. In the coming decades, when we are old and feeble, they will govern our world and control our lives. What kind of caregivers are we creating? What kind of healthcare decision-makers are we making? The Baby Boomers have been called the pampered generation or the smothered generation. However, it has become a generation of compassionate caregivers. What kind of caregivers are we creating among the neglected generation? Children without attachments become adults without a conscience. Reallocation of our national expenditures toward children now may someday protect our life, liberty and happiness. Regardless, they deserve a better world in which to grow.

CHAPTER ELEVEN

GLOBAL TRAVEL

An eleventh force that has already begun to change the healthcare delivery system is global travel.

Across the centuries, travel has been both a blessing and a curse. It has enabled the spread of knowledge, skills, personnel, and practices around the world. This has been especially true in the spread of medical information, medical people, and medical practices around the globe.

When the Greeks conquered the Middle East, they introduced "professional" medicine (such as it was) to their known world. When Rome conquered Greece, officers took Greek physicians across Europe, Africa, and the Middle East. In the first century A.D., a physician traveled with a man named Paul. His recording of so many stories about the "Great Physician" gave the practice of medicine "Divine Approval." Thus, monasteries also became hospitals. Universities founded to train clergy became institutions that also trained doctors. Missionaries sent to establish churches worldwide eventually included medical missionaries to establish hospitals around the globe.

Modern worldwide travel and the speed at which people, supplies, equipment, and technology can now move have enabled medicine to go around the world overnight. On

August 12, 2000, on a plane from Atlanta to San Diego a group of approximately twenty people rode together. They were members of a "medical" missionary team—physicians, nurses, dentists, therapists, technicians, electricians, contractors, plumbers, carpenters, teachers, ministers, and spouses. They had taken an eight-day "vacation" at their own expense to a village in Africa where they worked twenty-hour days. They flew out of Africa that morning to get back home in San Diego by dark.

The speed that modern jets, ships, trains, cars, and trucks can move medical people, supplies, equipment, and services around the globe is exciting and encouraging. Today the delivery of basic medicine is possible within days anywhere in the world, and in many places it is a matter of hours. New technology and improvements will enable planes to fly faster and farther and land in more remote locations. New ships will be bigger and faster and be able to dock in small harbors or even on beaches at remote islands. Rail service will be standardized, modernized, and globalized.

Delivering healthcare to the world will no longer be the problem. Global travel will make it possible.

Global travel will also have its deadly side. While global travel has taken medical miracles around the world, it has also taken medical disasters around the world. Global travel has spread and will enable the spread of disease, plagues, bacteria, and viruses to every corner of the world.

Historically, great plagues, such as the Bubonic Plague, Black Plague, smallpox, polio, and measles, have been transported from town to town, village to village, country to country. More recently, various strains of flu have been transported from continent to continent. Almost overnight, great plagues can now travel around the globe in a matter of hours. Perhaps there is no disease like AIDS that best illustrates the power of modern travel to transport a deadly virus. The virus is harmless within the indigenous monkeys of Africa. Africans, however, became infected with the virus. It has proved fatal to humans; and it spread around the world in a matter of months.

We know the individual who brought it to America. We know the day he flew into this country. We know the town in which he landed. It's called ground zero, day one, of the epidemic in this country.

On Wednesday, May 30, 2001, the *Wall Street Journal* carried a cover story entitled "Twenty Years of AIDS in America" (B1). In 1980 one person returned home from a trip to Africa and brought what would become known as AIDS to America. The very first scientific report about the disease appeared on June 5, 1981, in the *Mortality and Morbidity Weekly Report* of the Center for Disease Control.

Prior to that AIDS had already been discovered by medical missionaries in Africa who noticed an incurable illness that slowly wasted patients into skin-shrouded skeletons. Dr. Anne Bayley went to Zambia in 1961. She was an associate professor of medicine at the University Teaching Hospital in the Zambian capital of Lusaka. Her research and treatments soon connected the illness to a defect in the immune system. "Spotting AIDS in Africa Shaped Doctor's Destiny" read the headlines of a report by Mark Schoors, staff reporter of the *Wall Street Journal.*

In only twenty years, the disease has spread across Africa and around the world. In Africa alone the number of countries and people infected with AIDS is staggering:

1. Botswana — 35.80%
2. Zimbabwe — 25.06%
3. Zambia — 19.95%
4. South Africa — 19.94%
5. Namibia — 19.54%
6. Malawi — 15.96%
7. Kenya — 13.95%
8. Mozambique — 13.22%

9.	Rwanda	11.21%
10.	Ethiopia	10.63%
11.	Uganda	8.30%
12.	Tanzania	8.09%
13.	Ghana	3.60%

Notice that thirteen of the fourteen countries with the highest incidences of AIDS are all located in Africa. However, AIDS has infected the world. Below are listed other countries ranked by percentage of adults infected:

1.	Haiti	5.17%
2.	Dominican Republic	2.80%
3.	Thailand	2.15%
4.	Senegal	1.77%
5.	Ukraine	0.96%
6.	India	0.70%
7.	Argentina	0.69%
8.	United States	0.61%
9.	Spain	0.58%
10.	Brazil	0.57%
11.	Costa Rica	0.54%
12.	Switzerland	0.46%

The total worldwide death toll from AIDS has now reached 21.8 million! In the U.S., it is the leading cause of death for all Americans between the ages of twenty-five and forty-four. The number of Americans newly infected with the AIDS virus each year is 40,000. In twenty years, it has become a global epidemic.

On Saturday, August 5, 2000, CBS featured a fictional movie about a plane flying to London with a small cargo of top-secret, deadly bacteria similar to smallpox. The plane crashed and exploded. The contents were released and transmitted into the air. The unsuspecting clean-up crew and investigators were the first exposed. At the same time, all the passengers on all the flights leaving London for destinations around the world were also exposed.

Initially, experts were not even certain of the effects of the bacteria. The President of the United States was forced to make a difficult decision. Should he have all planes turn back to London? Some without enough fuel would crash in the ocean. It would cause worldwide panic. It would, however, give researchers more time to determine if the bacteria were a serious threat. Instead, he let the planes continue and land in cities around the globe, including the United States.

By the time the threat was determined to be real and deadly, planes had already landed worldwide. The president and top staff were flown to a protected island near Seattle. The rest of his family were at Duke University. They could not be rescued.

The Centers for Disease Control became the focal point of emergency research to find an antibody and a cure. Blood samples were brought into Atlanta. The C.D.C. was placed under heavy security, surrounded by the National Guard. Troops were called out all over the country as the uncontrolled epidemic spread.

One of the deadly vials was accidentally dropped in the laboratory at the C.D.C. headquarters, threatening the lives of all the researchers. They began to die, one by one.

That story may well illustrate what's ahead for our world. Almost prophetically it was aired thirteen months before September 11, 2001. Since then, the threat of anthrax and bioterrorism has become real, global, postal, and deadly. Apparently, a real bioterrorist dropped several letters—each containing enough anthrax to kill over 100,000 people—into a mailbox in New Jersey. They were sent to Senate Majority Leader Tom Daschle and Senator Patrick Leahy. Letters were also sent to the offices of the *Enquirer Magazine* and *NBC*. The deadly spores seeped out of the letters and contaminated equipment and other mail. Hundreds of people were exposed, scores of offices were contaminated, dozens of people were infected and five people were killed. An institution so noble and so useful as the U.S. Postal Service had become an instrument of deadly bioterrorism and mass murder.

This, along with the recent spread of SARS illustrates for us the new world order in which we live and the new world threats we now face. A new virus or bacteria, or more likely, a mutation of an old one, will be immune to current medical treatment and carried by mail, package, or unsuspecting traveler back home or to another country. Tourists, business travelers, researchers, political or military personnel, even medical people themselves could knowingly (because they are sick and want to come back to the best healthcare available) or unknowingly become infected and infect others while traveling. They continue their travels, return home, and infect someone else or others. This is especially true if the virus or bacteria is latent, has a dormant stage, or is airborne.

Blood-borne pathogens, such as AIDS, illustrate the incredible risk of global travel and worldwide epidemics. Yet, they pale in comparison to eurodenial pathogens, which are received and extricated through the digestive or reproductive system of the body. Worst of all are the pulmonary pathogens received and passed on through the air we breathe.

Global travel, for better or worse, will accelerate in the years ahead. Will "health detectors," like metal detectors, be employed in airports, seaports, and national checkpoints to "intercept" disease carriers in transit? Will health detectors be used at entrances to schools, malls, businesses, government centers, and sports and civic arenas to protect the public when assembling in large groups? What will O.S.H.A. require in order to provide a "safe" working environment and what will the courts allow? What will other countries do?

Twenty or fifty years from now, getting a "periodic health check up" or receiving a "clean bill of health" could mean something very different and have vastly different conse-quences from what it does today. Global travel is changing the healthcare arena and rewriting the rules of epidemiology.

It was this very issue that caused Congress to pass the very first national healthcare legislation in 1782! To protect cities and sailors along the seacoast from infectious diseases, Congress passed a law prohibiting U. S. Navy sailors from leaving a ship if they were sick or ships from docking where there were known epidemics. In this century, the U. S. Congress and the United Nations will face some similar but very difficult healthcare choices. Some of these are caused by global travel.

CHAPTER TWELVE

❧

MEDICAL MUTATION

A twelfth force changing the healthcare delivery system is the impact of medical mutations. Advances in medicine are creating new ways to live and new ways to die. The old plagues of the ninteenth and twentieth centuries have given way to the new plagues of the twenty-first century. *Business and Health*, the *Wall Street Journal*, the *New England Journal of Medicine*, *Business Week*, *Newsweek*, *Time*, *Consumer Reports*, and *U. S. News and World Report* are reporting on a frightening new phenomenon—super killers.

The new medical mutations have been called "super diseases," "super germs," "super viruses," or "super bacteria." *Consumer Reports*, in its January 2001 issue, described the once "long-simmering problem of antibiotic-resistant" bacteria as "nearing the boiling point."

According to the article, "More than two-thirds of the bacterial infections acquired in U. S. hospitals and about half of the common bacterial infections in outpatients do not respond to at least one of the antibiotics that used to work. For the first time, there are now five types of bacteria with strains resistant to all available antibodies" (p.60).

55

According to an article in *U. S. Today* (4-18-01, p. 60), "Infections caused by germs that resist treatment with antibiotics kill more than 14,000 Americans each year." Dr. Richard Roberts, president of the American Academy of Family Physicians, says, "It is estimated that 50 million antibiotic prescriptions for illnesses such as cold or flu are given each year and are of no benefit." In fact, this practice is deadly because it is creating highly resistant bacteria and increasingly weakened immune systems.

Many factors have contributed to this crisis. Half the people who have ever lived are alive today. They are huddled closer together, living longer, and working in tighter environments with less fresh air. They breathe more recycled air and less fresh air. They drink more recycled water or bottled water from increasingly contaminated sources. They eat prepared foods processed by people with more illnesses, viruses and diseases in places with more contaminates.

Moreover, they receive healthcare treatments in offices where they are exposed to sicker patients. They receive medical treatment in outpatient facilities that see people only hospital emergency rooms would handle twenty years ago. If they go to the hospital, only the sickest of the sick are there, and they are sent home before they are "well" to expose other family members to increasingly resistant germs, bacteria, viruses, and diseases.

Other factors contribute to the problem of medical mutation. We consume water treated with bacteria-fighting agents. We eat foods treated with bacteria-fighting agents or eat animal or agricultural products, which were treated with antibiotics. Even the use of antibacterial cleaners may be contributing to a new generation of super germs sond super viruses.

However, the biggest cause, according to the Food and Drug Administration, "one that patients can help control, is the medical misuse or overuse of antibiotics" (*Consumer Reports*, p.60). Researchers estimate that nearly half of the prescriptions written outside of hospitals are inappropriate. Sometimes the antibiotic is administered when not necessary or not even appropriate.

A coalition of federal and private groups met in Washington on April 17, 2001, to launch an educational campaign called "Save Antibiotic Strength." It was launched first in California, Virginia, and Connecticut to raise awareness of the over prescription and misuse of antibiotics.

Pressure on physicians, often by patients themselves, to prescribe "something" pushes harried physicians to give an antibiotic. Sometimes the wrong antibiotic is prescribed. Inadequate tests, inaccurate diagnoses, or over-the-phone requests can prompt antibiotic misuse.

And many times antibiotics are overused. Physicians recommend plenty of bed rest and lots of fluids for the common cold or flu, and aspirin for pain. Even low-grade fever is a part of the body's attempt to slow us down and create temperatures that kill many viral infections. However, patients complain, "Doc, I don't have time for bed rest. Give me some medicine instead. I've got to keep going." Pediatricians often hear, "Doc, give us an antibiotic for my child. I've got to get him (or her) well enough to go back to the child care/school so I can get back to work."

The increased pressure on physicians and hospitals to treat more patients in less time, with pre-approved medications and formularies and fewer tests, often pushes people back to work/school/child care more quickly. Again, healthy people are being exposed to more unhealthy people. More powerful medications are then used and misused to keep the population going, especially in the winter months.

Thus, managing healthcare by plan design and payor control is fostering an environment ripe for epidemics. Modern mutations—super viruses, super diseases—will kill us unless we transform the way we deliver illness care and the way we provide healthcare.

CHAPTER THIRTEEN

❧

LIFESTYLES

Another major force driving up the cost of healthcare in America is unhealthy lifestyles. There are at least ten major life style choices that people make which are negatively impacting healthcare and driving up the costs for all Americans.

1. Smoking

In 1977, Joseph Califano had the courage, and some called it the audacity, to release and present to Congress a study done by his young deputy assistant, C. Everett Koop. The study revealed the deadly dangers of smoking. Less than six months later, under intense political pressure, Califano and his deputy assistant were replaced. However, the study became a landmark. Clearly the tobacco industry and the states that earned a great deal of money from the sale of tobacco forced the resignations, but the landmark information confirmed what Americans were already beginning to sense with overwhelming evidence that smoking was the number-one health problem in America.

2. Drinking

Here is an industry that has created a national health and humanitarian nightmare and yet has dodged major political and press criticism. It borders on the amazing and even astonishing. How the use and abuse of alcohol have been largely ignored by the press, Congress, and even attorneys is unbelievable. It is amazing, even astonishing, how smoking could incur the wrath of politicians, press, attorneys and the public and how the use and abuse of alcohol can be almost totally ignored.

Perhaps it is because most political, media, and medical professionals drink; or it is because so many liquor industry advertising dollars are invested in the media; or perhaps because of the amount of political contributions given by the distillery industry. Perhaps the reason the liquor industry has avoided political and legal condemnation is a result of the aftermath of prohibition. Some would suggest it has avoided political, media, and legal criticism because of the enormous influence of the Kennedys who made their money from the sale of alcohol; or it is ignored because of the Mob and how it continues to make its money through the distribution of alcohol and related activities. Whatever the reason, the major health and humanitarian problems created by alcohol has been minimized and kept out of the public limelight.

Only Mothers Against Drunk Driving, Students Against Drunk Driving, and the American Medical Association have raised public concern about alcohol and its related problems.

Considering all of its many facets, drinking may be the number-one health problem in America. Certainly, drinking and driving and the number of automobile accidents, fatalities, and injuries that occur because someone has been using alcohol is well documented and the tragic stories are often publicized. However, equally frightening are the number of accidents on the job and at home caused by drinking.

Even obesity (especially among young people) can be associated with the consumption of beer and alcohol. Perhaps most of all is the direct relationship between drinking and violence. In most cases, drinking is involved in cases of domestic violence, public violence, sexual abuse, spousal abuse, child abuse, rape, robbery, and assault.

3. Drugs—The Use and Abuse of Legal and Illegal Drugs

Certainly, there is an enormous health and humanitarian cost related to the trafficking, selling, distributing, use of, and lifestyle behavior associated with illegal drug use. But add to that the high cost of legal drug use, over-the-counter medications, misuse of over-the-counter drugs to help us go to sleep, wake up, lose weight, gain weight, eliminate pain, fight colds, and make us look better.

The fastest growing component of healthcare plans driving up the cost of healthcare is prescriptions, accounting for as much as 15 percent of all healthcare costs.

4. Promiscuity

A behavior pattern contributing to the increasing cost of healthcare is the catching and spreading of sexually transmitted diseases (STDs) including AIDS. According to the Center for Disease Control, there are at least twenty-five sexually transmitted diseases, four of which have **no** cure. What is shocking to young people who have been conditioned to believe that condoms provide safe sex is that they are only 75 percent effective at best. That is they are only 75 percent effective *when used properly*. Most are not. They are not always used 100 percent of the time, seldom used in oral sex, and only occasionally used in anal sex, all of which allow for the transmission of sexually transmitted diseases, especially AIDS. Condoms do not cover all exposed areas and may slide off.

In addition to the sexually transmitted diseases related to promiscuity, a number of unwanted pregnancies that occur may lead to abortions, abandoned children, unwanted children, abused children, or children born in poverty, which perpetuate poor health and numerous other demands on our health and human service system.

5. Major Medical Nightmares

There are three medical or health plan nightmares:
(1) Neonatal intensive care
(2) Medical intensive care
(3) Surgical intensive care

Medical intensive care relates to brain injuries and a person remaining in a Medical Intensive Care Unit in a coma caused by a stroke or accident.

Surgical intensive care can result from major accidents that have multiple internal injuries. Multiple or complicated transplants or surgeries can also lead to long stays in Surgical Intensive Care Units.

Neonatal intensive care is usually the result of premature, physically impaired newborns. It is the most frequent, the most costly, and yet the most avoidable intensive care unit expense. With good prenatal care, mothers can usually carry babies longer, usually to term—resulting in healthier babies, higher birth weight, fewer abnormalities, and shorter stays in hospital nursing units.

Certainly one of the complications of fertility procedures is multiple births. Multiple births almost always produce premature children. The cost of a premature baby can range between $100,000 and $250,000. It is easy to see why when someone has quintuplets they can run up million-dollar medical bills.

6. Obesity

Here is a topic that is very volatile and politically incorrect to discuss because so many people are overweight. There is an increasing percentage of obesity in our population. Over 25 percent of all children are seriously overweight and are clinically diagnosed as obese, defined as 30 percent over their normal body weight. As a result, their obesity increases the likelihood of diabetes, high blood pressure, heart attack and other cardiovascular problems and complications, a decline in the immune system, pulmonary problems, skeletal problems (especially back, hip, and knee problems), kidney problems, digestive abnormalities or difficulties, sexual dysfunction, and the need for increasing amounts of medications. Trying to find appropriate combinations of medications that do not have a serious number of side effects for the obese patient is very frustrating for physicians and very expensive for health plans.

7. Degree of Inactivity

Inactivity and the lack of exercise certainly contribute to obesity. However, the sedentary lifestyle and lack of exercise also creates weakness in the muscular system, the cardiovascular system, the respiratory system, the digestive system, the kidney system, the renal system, and the immune system.

8. Overactivity

For all those that are inactive, there are also those that are overactive. They have overprogrammed their own lives and the lives of their children; they are over-scheduled, overworked, and overcommitted. They work too much, play too much, and spend too much. They get little rest. They are often drowsy when working and worse when driving. They lack time to relax and unwind and often resort to self-medication or other medications. They may use drugs and alcohol to keep going; then use drugs and alcohol to relax and unwind. They often lack recreation, so they do not get the right kind of activity—cardiovascular, muscular, skeletal— to help restore the body to full health and to make all of the systems function properly.

9. Stress

A lifestyle issue that increases healthcare costs is the stress-filled lives many people lead. This often results from the need to succeed or accumulate. Thus, there is a significant amount of financial stress in our culture.

Ten percent of America's workforce is being threatened with legal action every day. Another 30 percent of America's workforce is faced with creditor action and are behind in at least one major payment. Another 30 percent of the workforce can only make the minimum payments. Hence, 70 percent of America's workforce is facing significant financial difficulties and is under severe financial stress.

Add to this the occupational stressors— downsizing, mergers, acquisitions, doing more with less, job re-engineering, corporate re-engineering, global travel, and a new one called "technology entanglement." People are working 24/7 and are connected twenty-four hours a day, seven days a week. Whether officially at work or on vacation or at home via the Internet, they are connected to work (entangled), through phones, laptops, and pagers. There is no such thing as "time off."

Then there is relational stress—conflicts with a spouse, parents, children, siblings, relatives, friends, boss, colleagues, or competitors. Some people have even added the stress of trying to have a lover or liaison outside of marriage. Others have the added stress caused by multiple partners.

There is social stress from relocations, activities, belonging to clubs, associations, churches, and the increasing demands that are placed on people because of their social commitments.

And then there is cultural stress. Society in general is running at a much higher pace with information overload. The industrialized world is functioning in high gear with its high-tech lifestyle, hard living, road rage, mall madness, air rage, Internet anxiety, identity theft—and then after September 11th, the whole fear of terrorism.

Stress reduces our immune system, creates difficulties for our cardio-vascular system, neurological system, skeletal system, and digestive system and may increase the risk of cancer, strokes, heart attacks, and diabetes.

10. Stupidity

Yes, I hate to use the word, but it relates to high-risk behavior that does not make good sense:
   (1) Not wearing seat belts and shoulder straps
   (2) Drinking and driving
   (3) Drowsy driving
   (4) Distracted driving (using cell phones and CD players, eating or reading while driving)
   (5) Speeding
   (6) Using drugs

(7) Promiscuity

(8) Some people might add other high risk behaviors such as riding motorcycles, skateboarding, bull riding, hang gliding, bungee jumping, rock climbing, rappelling—to name a few

All of these behaviors can create major trauma injuries. These injuries impact young people especially, because they tend to take greater risks and have a sense of immortality that prompts them to do things that wisdom and age discourages. When severely injured, they must then live with the results for a lifetime.

These life-changing injuries extract a major toll on medical plans, require workplace accommodations, and often have medical complications that will follow the person for the rest of their lives. Unfortunately, all of us have done some of those things, especially when we were young and felt invincible, and we have medical injuries that occasionally require medical treatment. If we could get every person to wear seatbelts, stop drinking and driving, speeding, using drugs, and driving while drowsy, then a significant amount of medical expenses could be reduced or eliminated.

CHAPTER FOURTEEN

❧

OVERCAPITALIZATION

A fourteenth force that's changing healthcare for the coming decades is overcapitalization. It is in many ways a "Catch 22." There are too many hospitals, too many hospital beds, too many hospital rooms, too many physician offices, too many administrators, and too many stockholders. Yet at the same time, the nature of healthcare reimbursement and the demands of consumers are driving the industry to increase capital expenditures. Thus, the industry is forced to even greater overcapitalization.

There are simply too many beds. In 1990 a study was released indicating that half the beds in the United States would no longer be needed by the year 2000. Today most hospitals are barely over 50 percent occupied. Though some of the rooms have been converted into offices or other uses, the amount of capital remains the same, while at the same time, hospitals have spent major dollars on outpatient surgical complexes.

Of the rooms available, many are antiquated, out-dated, and in drastic need of revitalization and remodeling. Many of the buildings were built forty or fifty years ago. The funding that was made available in the 1940s for hospital expansion and hospital creation have now created far too much capacity.

67

The overall cost of simply bringing *all* hospitals up to competitive standards means spending *trillions* of dollars.

There are too many hospitals with expensive equipment, and in many geographical areas there is multiple duplication of services and facilities. This is especially true in metropolitan communities. Meanwhile, in rural areas hospitals have disappeared.

In metropolitan areas, hospitals are under enormous pressure to upgrade and have the latest and greatest of everything. In fact, the pressure is on to have *more* than the competition. There is immense pressure to be high-tech. The cost of having the latest and greatest high-tech often comes at the expense of high-touch. So, it is the staffing on the units that has been dramatically cut—almost dangerously cut. There is pressure to have more technology and fewer people.

What has occurred in most major hospitals has been a dramatic expenditure in outpatient surgical suites so that patients can come in and out in twenty-three hours. Hospital outpatient suites have become the equivalent of "fast food" in the healthcare industry.

A number of factors have driven this continuous press to overcapitalization: cost-plus pricing, percentage billing, and cost shifting. Many emergency rooms have become free clinics for the financially disenfranchised and for persons without healthcare coverage; thus, creating emergency rooms where paying customers are reluctant to go. This has created a further capitalization of healthcare—medical office complexes and suburban emergency centers. Emergency care centers are springing up in suburbs around cities, skimming off the self-paying and leaving the emergency rooms of major hospitals to be fully functional 24/7 with many no-pay patients. Also, private surgical suites are beginning to emerge in suburban areas taking self-paying patients or well-paying third-party patients away from the surgical suites of hospitals. This has created a cash-flow problem and a long-term capitalization problem.

Another example of the overcapitalization is too many physicians' office buildings and suites. No longer does a physician have an office; they usually have a high-tech, state-of-the-art suite or building. This means a larger and larger percentage of their income must be used to sustain an ever-increasing overhead. Most physician office complexes operate with 50 percent to 80 percent overhead. They have become capital-intensive facilities with many expensive exam rooms, laboratories, and high-tech equipment—once found only in hospitals. Somebody must pay for all of this.

Another growing example of this overcapitalization problem is the close geographical proximity of civilian hospitals, military hospitals, and veteran administration hospitals. Some of the civilian hospitals are private or for profit facilities; others are not-for-profit. In our community within a ten-mile radius, there are four freestanding hospitals, representing three different medical systems with intense competition to have all the latest and greatest of equipment and to have more than the competition. At the same time, there is a major military facility that needs millions of dollars to bring it up to standard—let alone prepare it for the thirty to forty years ahead. So the military, especially in the United States and particularly in populated areas, is facing a significant financial quandary to determine whether it is going to invest the billions of dollars necessary to bring its hospitals up to standard and compete with the private sector or to create partnerships with private or not-for-profit civilian hospitals.

The final aspect of overcapitalization is too many stockholders in healthcare. There are too many investors from third-party administrators, insurance companies, hospitals, physicians, service providers, and other investors who want an above-average return on their investment.

There is a fundamental difference between the manufacturing and service industries—especially a labor-intensive service industry. Manufacturing can show a greater profit margin through mass production, process simplification, and product substitution. In the service industry, which is labor-intensive, economies of scale are marginal and there is only a limited amount of product substitution acceptable. Hence, it is indeed very difficult to squeeze profit out of mass production in the service industry, especially when it comes to healthcare.

Chapter Fifteen

THE ILLNESS SYSTEM

Another force driving us to a new healthcare solution is our current illness system. In America we do not have a healthcare system. We have an *illness care system.* There is little or nothing about our current system that rewards people for being healthy or for choosing a healthy lifestyle. The whole payment system, whether provided by the government or through the insurance industry, is a "use it or lose it" system.

Medical spending accounts are designed to either use it or lose it. Insurance coverage is the same way. Either use the benefit or lose it. Medical or health insurance is like term life insurance. It provides coverage for the "term" of the agreement. However, the premiums paid are not recovered unless you are sick. The whole system covers you if you get sick. It's a sick care or illness care system. It pays little or nothing to people to stay healthy. It pays only if a person is sick, and the sicker a person is, the more it pays. With large deductibles, the system pays nothing if people have only minor injuries or are rarely sick. Co-payments mean that the insurer will pay 80 percent and the patient will pay 20 percent if he is occasionally or minimally sick. However, if a person is chronically ill and has continuous illness problems and reaches his out-of-pocket limit, then the plan pays ***100 percent*** of ***all*** medical expenses and the patient no longer has any out-of-pocket expense. So, the sicker you are the more it pays, the more things you have done, the more the health plan covers. Thus, our "healthcare system" is not a healthcare system; it is an illness treatment system. The sicker one becomes, the more it pays. The healthier one remains, the less it pays.

There are some plans that pay for preventive programs. They will pay 100 percent for pap smears, mammograms, prostate screenings, and annual physicals, although they have age limitations. Unfortunately, these plans are usually limited to only the best plans. The weaker healthcare plan or illness treatment plans pay very little, if any, for preventive programs. Even fewer plans pay for wellness programs.

I know of no plan that pays you not to smoke, drink, do drugs, maintain an optimum body weight, participate in an exercise program, or attend healthcare education. Very few plans pay for healthcare education, let alone for people to attend them. Certainly few plans pay you to use seatbelts and wear helmets.

When it comes to mental health services, the majority of plans are still illness-oriented. Most people have to be given a clinical diagnosis (psychological illness) in order to access mental health services. A healthy mind facilitates a healthy body. Most plans provide very, very limited mental health services. Certainly very few plans pay 80 percent to 100 percent of counseling for work/life issues or provide for life coaching, skill building, or relationship sustaining.

Few plans pay for complementary medicine, vitamin supplements, nutrient supplements, health and wellness retreats, or marriage and family retreats. So again, almost all plans are designed to pay for illness and pay nothing for wellness.

Even fewer plans have sanctions for people who live what was referred to earlier as the "death wish" lifestyles. These people, because of their lifestyle choices, seem to wish for death sooner than others by engaging in behavior such as smoking, drinking, using drugs, promiscuity, obesity, inactivity, not wearing seat belts, and drinking and driving. People participating in "death wish" lifestyles or "death styles" are rarely penalized for their poor choices.

As a nation we cannot continue to reward people's unhealthy lifestyle choices and fail to reward conscientious people who engage in healthy activities and health building programs. In fifty years, this nation has gone from spending 3 percent of our gross domestic product (GDP) on illness services to spending 15 percent of the GDP. At this pace, in fifty years it will be 75 percent of the GDP—75 percent of all the money we make as a nation will go to illness care. That is 75 percent of our salaries, 75 percent of company revenues and 75 percent of the federal, state, and local budgets.

A telling statistic reflecting our backward focus comes from 1978, during Jimmy Carter's administration when Joseph Califano was Secretary of Health, Education, and Welfare. This country spent $250 **billion** in "illness" care and spent $400 **million** on wellness and prevention programs. In 2000, we spent $1.2 **trillion** on "illness" care in this country and yet we still spent only $400 **million** on wellness and prevention programs. Something is terribly wrong with this picture.

Clearly we must start doing something to encourage people to be healthy and reward people for being healthy. Moreover, we must make it less attractive for people to choose destructive "death styles" and discourage the excessive use of our "illness treatment" system. In addition, when people are healthy and stay healthy, the money they save needs to be carried forward and not lost so that they are not punished for being healthy. The time is now for healthcare savings accounts that are tax exempt, roll forward, and are portable.

❧

Chapter Sixteen

Medical Industrial Complex

The medical industrial complex is the sixteenth force driving us to a new healthcare delivery system. What is the medical industrial complex? How does it function? How does it put extra pressure on the economy of the United States? How is it part of the problem? Can it be a part of the solution?

First, perhaps, we need to answer the question "What is the medical industrial complex?" It is all of the institutions, organizations, and individuals that benefit from the $1.6 *trillion* healthcare industry, or more accurately stated, the illness-treatment industry. It is anyone or any organization that has anything to do, directly or indirectly, with healthcare. It is all hospitals, laboratories, offices, and clinics. It is all health-related doctors, lawyers, nurses, clinicians, therapists, technicians, teachers, administrators, and staff. It is all pharmaceutical companies, pharmacies, insurance companies, medical supply companies, medical equipment companies, third-party administrators, and reinsurers. It is all construction companies, architects, vendors, suppliers of administrative services, and banks that provide anything related to healthcare facilities or providers.

The medical industrial complex is all patients, relatives, politicians, and regulators. It is all government entities that receive healthcare related funds, provide medical property, and receive tax revenues from physicians and for-profit hospitals. It is also stockholders of healthcare-related business. It is all third-party payors. It is all businesses and organizations that use healthcare benefits as a competitive edge to attract good employees. It is unions who use healthcare benefits as a key leverage to justify union membership. So it is all of these plus other institutions, organizations, and individuals that benefit from the over $1.6 *trillion* illness-treatment industry.

A phrase emerged in the 1960s called the "military industrial complex." It grew out of concern regarding the 1960s Viet Nam War. The questions raised especially in the late 1960s, were: Whose war is this? Why are we fighting? For whom are we fighting? Who is winning? Who is losing? Who is benefiting from this twelve-year on-going war? People began to question the motives behind the war and the growing concern that the only winners in all of this were the industries that made money on waging war. They were the ones who supplied all the war material. In the end, it seemed that the war was about sustaining the military industrial complex.

So the same question is being raised about the illness treatment industry: Who benefits the most from the system we have in place? In fact, this industry is even bigger than the $1.6 *trillion* when one factors in all of the other industries that benefit from the current system as it is. Perhaps there are those who don't want to fix the current system. Perhaps they prefer an illness treatment system. Too many people, too many organizations, and too many institutions benefit from an industry focused almost exclusively on the *treatment* of illnesses. Maybe too many people really do not want to cut costs. Maybe they really do not want to have a less expensive system. Maybe they really do not want a *healthcare* system. Maybe they really do not want people to be healthy.

Thus, the one great big question remains: Who is going to pay for it? Who will pay for an ever-increasing, very expensive illness treatment system? Who will pay for an ever-increasing, very expensive aging population? Who will bear the financial burden?

In 1950, only 3 percent of the gross domestic output or gross domestic product was used to sustain the healthcare industry. By the year 2000, 14 percent of our gross domestic output was consumed by illness treatment. Moreover, there has been an increasing number of takers and decreasing number of givers to fund the current illness treatment system. This will be especially true when the Baby Boomer generation hits retirement. By the year 2010, half of the population of the United States will be over fifty. Who will pay for the extraordinary medical liability that all of these people will place on our healthcare delivery system? Who will sustain the medical industrial complex? Who will sustain the illness treatment demands of an aging population?

The high cost of maintaining the medical industrial complex and the ever-increasing number of people making demands upon it are driving us to a new paradigm—a new healthcare delivery system.

CHAPTER SEVENTEEN

BIOGENETIC ENGINEERING

Another force driving us to reconsider the current illness paradigm and shift to a new one is the complications of biogenetic engineering.

Biogenetic engineering has many forms. We know that genes determine the make up of individuals. We know that genes determine risk factors. Now, we know the genes that determine people at high risk. The questions currently being debated are: Do we perform genetic testing to determine risk factors for high-risk people? Will the results have an impact on coverage, cost, employment, and treatment?

Biogenetic re-engineering allows for the re-engineering of genetic makeup, which changes the outcome of the individual. Re-engineering individuals means restructuring the genetic pool. Re-engineering the genetic pools means restructuring the population. Re-engineering allows us even at this point to redetermine the outcome of the egg or embryo, and now re-engineering allows us to take stem cells and create replacement parts. So, it has enormous implications.

Cloning is but one of the crucial issues. Whose genetic makeup are we going to use? Will there ultimately be pressure to exclude some from the genetic pool and include others? Will we reach the point where we determine the ideal genetic makeup and construct it separately from or in conjunction with the current humans that exist at this time? And who pays for the cost of cloning?

The more practical applications and implications relate to infertility. Under the Americans with Disabilities Act, having children is a protected right—a basic life activity. To what extent will infertility treatment proceed? To what extent will biogenetic re-engineering be allowed? What about career couples who want to avoid disrupting their careers when having children? What about homosexual couples? What about individuals who want to have children genetically coded after themselves or after someone else? What about older people having children? These are some of the ethical questions.

Then what about the financial questions. Who will pay for it? The question is no longer what can be done, but what will it cost and who will pay for it?

This leads to even more controversial issues related to biogenetic engineering—the use of stem cells. Certainly biogenetic engineering of animals for their parts is a growing business. Will we start doing the same with humans—growing and harvesting stem cells for replacement parts, including spinal parts, limbs, hands, feet, hearts, kidneys, lungs, livers, eyes, ears, and even sexual organs? Again, it is no longer a question of what can be done, but what will it cost and who will pay. Under the current system, the thinking is "If it can be done, it's my right to have it. I'll sue to prove it and then someone else must pay for it."

Thus, biogenetic engineering *is* driving us to a new system for healthcare.

CHAPTER EIGHTEEN

ॐ

THE IMMORTALITY ILLUSION

Another force driving us to a new paradigm in healthcare is the immortality illusion. We somehow believe that death is avoidable. For some incredible reason, we believe we can postpone death *indefinitely*. We have the illusion that life continues on and on and on—the illusion that life comes without death attached to the end of it. We live as if we will live *forever*. We have the illusion that there are only two stages of life. You are born and then live…at least we seem to live that way.

Even more amazing is that we expect our healthcare system to keep us that way. We expect our healthcare, or our illness treatment system, to keep us alive, pain-free, functioning well and doing so *indefinitely*. We want to avoid death at all costs. We do not talk about death, plan for death, or make choices in light of death. Sometimes parents want to discuss their final arrangements, funerals, and wills with their adult children. The adult children, however, do not want to even hear about it. How many of us have made death plans? Do we have a will? Do we have a living will? Do we have a durable power of attorney for healthcare? Have we selected a gravesite?

Have we paid for it? Have we made funeral arrangements? Have we discussed them with our children or other relatives?

Usually, the answer to almost all of the above questions, especially for someone under age sixty-five is "No." Certainly when it comes to the choices about end-of-life decisions, most people have not spelled out what their choices would be. They have not even communicated to loved ones what their choices might be. When the time comes, many family members want extraordinary means used to sustain a body that is begging to be returned to the earth.

We accuse young people of having an immortality complex. They take extraordinary risks with their bodies and they believe they will not get hurt. If they are injured, they believe they will mend and be "as good as new." Adults have that same mentality in a different way. For some reason, death is a taboo subject about which people do not want to plan, talk, or make preparations. They live as if they will never die—as if death will never happen.

Few people have living wills and durable power of attorneys for healthcare. Suddenly something terrible happens. A person is on life support. The medical community is told, "Do all that you can." And there is a great deal they can do. The other situation is that of a terminally ill person. The medical community is asked, "Is there anything else you can do?" The answer is always "Yes," but the question is "Is it really life?"

We have a culture that fights age and death at all costs. Eighty percent of the healthcare dollar is spent on the last eighty days of life. Physicians have reported that 30 percent of all medical procedures are futile, a waste of time, money, and effort. Why? First, because our culture seems to prize the young, beautiful, and athletic, and it seems to increasingly devalue the old, wise, and elderly. It refuses to accept death as a natural part of life.

Certainly one of the factors that have contributed to this is how the medical world from 1940 to 1990 removed birth and death from life. Until 1940 most children were born in homes, and most adults died in their homes. For the first thirty years of the era, from 1940-1970, only doctors and nurses were invited into the labor and delivery room and the mother was covered from head to foot. She was not treated as a whole person. Thus, birth was separated from life.

Starting in 1970 the medical community allowed first the fathers and then other family members to participate in the birth process. In the last ten years, birthing suites have allowed more family members to join in the labor and delivery process. This seems to be reconnecting people to the cycle of life—birth to life to death. It also seems to be reconnecting people to where children ought to be born—not in a remote, sterile operating room but a birthing suite with an extended family.

In the last ten years, many ICU units have begun to allow family members greater access to dying patients and for longer periods of time. The advent of hospice is signaling a new day, a new age, and a new attitude in our culture. Fewer people are dying sedated and isolated in a hospital ward, but instead at home with dignity, surrounded by family and friends.

The clergy must share major responsibility for failing to help our culture to live and die. There was a time when we preached and taught people to get ready for the "final passage." Many of the older hymns in our hymnbooks conclude with a verse relating to "crossing the river on life's final journey." In recent years, however, our hymns have avoided what is unavoidable. Clergy over the past thirty years have not adequately helped people live noble lives and die noble deaths.

So the question remains "Is the immortality illusion driving us to a new paradigm in healthcare?" The answer is "Yes," and the solution may be found in the words of Solomon who wrote, "There is a time to be born and a time to die."

ɪ

HEALTHCARE AS AN ENTITLEMENT

The sense of entitlement to illness treatment is another force driving us to a revolution in healthcare. Before 1940, few people acted as if they felt entitled to healthcare. Certainly, there was little expectation that you were entitled to the best healthcare available and someone else must pay for it. From 1850 to 1880, the family provided healthcare at home. The closest thing to a pharmacist was the traveling medicine man or woman. People basically got whatever healthcare was provided by their family and perhaps their neighbors. There was certainly no expectation that the government would provide healthcare or even that neighbors were responsible for treating one's illness. If they came and helped, it was out of the goodness of their hearts, and they took enormous risks in so doing.

From 1880 to 1910 a community doctor provided healthcare. Communities, as indicated earlier, often would hire a teacher and a doctor. The "school" was the church. The doctor lived above his/her office and made house calls. People got whatever the doctor could give and the doctor got whatever the people could give. Again, there was little or no expectation that the government was to provide healthcare or that the neighbors or community were responsible or obligated

85

to provide "the best available" healthcare in the world. It was a collaborative community effort for which everyone seemed genuinely grateful.

From 1910 to 1940 with the rise of the industrial revolution and larger employers, companies started providing some form of healthcare for their employees. The factory would provide a clinic; perhaps hire a doctor to serve the employees and their families. Employees got what the clinic offered. Family members could use the services. Others in the community had access to that healthcare only through the kindness and generosity of the employer.

As the years passed, and the obvious disparity between what the employers were providing for the employees versus what the communities were providing to everyone else prompted more and more companies to give the company clinic to the community. But again, there was little or no expectation that people in the community were entitled with inalienable rights to access these company-owned and company-sponsored clinics.

The 1940s changed all of this. The passage of the Hill-Burton Act provided federal funds to communities to build and provide community hospitals. While the government would help build the hospitals, people still received what they could afford, or what the employer would pay for through insurers. Employees purchased insurance, providers submitted claims, and insurers processed the claims.

The federal government started providing coverage for government employees and then through government funds to those who fell into other populations—the Social Security population (ultimately called "Medicare") and then the uninsured, impoverished, and economically disadvantaged ("Medicaid" as it would eventually be called). Still, illness treatment was basically what these organizations would reimburse to providers after they submitted their claims for reimbursement. A subtle shift, however, was beginning.

In the 1960s and 1970s, a whole new sense of entitlement emerged. First from those who were paying taxes, then from those who were covered under federal programs. People felt entitled to government programs. In the last decade, the sense of entitlement has spread not only to every American citizen, but also to every non-citizen in this country, including illegal aliens. Many believe that they, too, should have access to any and all of the same healthcare that all American citizens have, regardless of costs. It is an interesting shift in fifty years—from little to no expectation to universal expectation or from an employment privilege to universal entitlement.

Compare this to the attitude people hold toward the other six necessities outlined in Abraham Maslow's *Hierarchy of Needs*. We all need air to breathe—a biological necessity. We all want clean air. There is an expectation that the government will help protect the air—for example through legislation such as the Clean Air Act—and even administer sanctions against major air polluters. But, when it comes to the major source of pollution in our culture, we have been reluctant to expect government to do whatever it takes and use punitive actions toward those who pollute. Of course, I am talking about cars— the major source of pollution in our culture and especially around our cities—cars, trucks, buses, etc. We have been reluctant to assert that inside a public building, including restaurants and other places, we have an inalienable right and entitlement to clean air. We still have sections for more contaminated air (smoking) and less contaminated air (non-smoking).

The second necessity is water. We all want clean water. We all expect that the water from municipalities will be clean and safe. However, access to water is not viewed as an entitlement. Access to quality water comes through a public utility. If we cannot pay for our water, it will be cut off. There is no sanction against the company or the utility for cutting off our water if we fail to pay for it. They are not sued for restricting or limiting the amount of water we can use if we cannot pay.

The third necessity is food. We all want good food. Here again is one of those necessities that we must purchase. There is an expectation that we will pay for it. Access to quality food is not seen as an entitlement. The only free food available is generally through charitable organizations. We do not expect or have a sense of entitlement or assume that the government will provide food for all of us or provide the same food for all of us. Of course, school programs are available, but you simply cannot walk into a grocery store or a restaurant and expect that they will provide you the same food they expect their other customers to pay for.

Clothes are another necessity. We all want nice clothes, but we understand that we must pay for them. The only free clothes are those that one might find at Goodwill or Salvation Army. Generally, one must pay a little something even for those. We do not expect to be able to walk into a department store or clothing store and demand the same items that everyone else is *buying* and wearing.

Another necessity is shelter. We all want shelter. We all would like to live in a nice home. However, we understand that we must pay for the shelter in which we live. Either we rent or buy shelter. The only free shelter is generally provided by charities. In fact, the government will actually leave people on the street without shelter. There is no sense of entitlement that everybody must be sheltered by the government. We certainly have no expectation that we can walk into a hotel or motel and demand that they provide us the same shelter for the night they are providing paying customers. We do not believe that everyone is entitled to the same quality of housing, regardless of one's ability to pay. People who can pay more get better housing.

Safety is something that we want and need. It is a necessity. We expect, to some degree, that the government will provide a safe environment in which we can live, work, and play. We do get upset when we believe our government is not doing enough to "keep our streets safe." However, if we feel unsafe, there is no sense of entitlement that we can simply call the government and demand that they come and make us feel safe inside and outside our homes, day or night, anywhere, anytime. There is no way that we can sue our government if we are injured and then expect them to restore us and make us whole. We certainly cannot sue the government for compensatory damages (for pain and suffering), nor can we sue the government for punitive damages—punishing the government for not keeping us safe and secure at all times and in all places.

Yet, when it comes to medicine, people think differently. People not only want to live healthy and pain-free lives, they have come to expect it and even demand it. Many people think that regardless of their circumstances, they can walk into an emergency room of a public or private medical facility, a charitable or private medical facility, and expect—and even demand—that they receive the same level of treatment as anyone else in society. And if they do not get it, they can sue those providers. They can sue not only for economic damages, but for compensatory and punitive damages, as well. In other words, they can punish the provider for not providing what they wanted, when they wanted it, where they wanted it, regardless of their ability to pay. This amazing sense of entitlement now has a political system that encourages it and a legal system that protects it and promotes it.

The question is "Have we created a monster?" Have we created an illness treatment system that every person of every age and of every station in life feels **entitled** to, and even has the force of law to make what is available to some now available to all? What is available to anyone must now be available to everyone and someone else must pay for it. Imagine the same mentality, philosophy, and legal force if it were imposed on food, water, clothes, or homes.

Take some examples:

Housing. If one person in a community has a ten-bedroom home with a swimming pool and tennis court, the entitlement mentality would dictate/legislate that everyone must receive the same treatment, the same services, the same facilities regardless of one's lifestyle or ability to pay.

Clothing. If any one person wears something, then every person should be entitled to the same clothing. Someone else should pay for it. A person can walk into Macy's and expect, even demand, anything anyone else has bought. If she doesn't get it, she can sue the owner.

Food. If one person eats in an expensive restaurant then everyone should be entitled to the same, and someone else must pay for it. If not, the restaurant operator would be sued for damages in a class-action suit on behalf of everyone who has ever been denied access to food.

Transportation. If someone drives a certain type of automobile, then everyone is entitled to drive the same type of automobile and someone else should pay for it.

What would happen to the country if the entitlement philosophy of illness treatment were applied to all seven necessities? The implications for the next century—even for the next decade—would be enormous. The entitlement philosophy of illness treatment is driving us to a new system altogether.

CHAPTER TWENTY

POPULATION OVERLOAD

The exponential growth in the world's population is another force driving the healthcare revolution.

Directly related to the aging population is the exponential growth of the earth's population. Consider this (*Time* magazine, October 18, 1999, p. 60):

It took 10,000 years to reach 1 billion people 1804
It took 123 years to reach 2 billion people 1927
It took 33 years to reach 3 billion people 1960
It took 14 years to reach 4 billion people 1974
It took 13 years to reach 5 billion people 1987
It took 12 years to reach 6 billion people 1999

It took millions of years to fill the planet with the first one billion people. Then it took only 123 years to add another billion. However, we tripled that amount, adding four billion people in seventy-three years! More alarming is the fact that over half the people who have ever lived—*ever*—are alive today! The entire world's population just one hundred years ago equals what one country (China) has today! By 2050,

India will have over 1.5 billion people, and in one hundred years India will have more people than China.

In just fifty years, twenty-six cities in the world will have over 10 million people each, including:

Hong Kong	Atlanta	Miami	New Orleans
Calcutta	Moscow	New York	Rio de Janeiro
Tokyo	London	Chicago	Mexico City
Detroit	Paris	Washington	Los Angeles
Singapore	St. Louis	San Francisco	

Most alarming of all is what the projected population of the world will be by the end of **this** century. By 2100, the population of the world will be between

12 billion and 24 billion!

By 2100, the population of this planet will have increased to between 12 and 24 billion people. The difference between these two projections comes from the annualized growth projection rate used:

Time Period	Annualized Rate of Growth	Projected
1998-2000	1%	12 billion
1960-2000	2%	18 billion
1900-2000	3%	24 billion

Thus, the *low-end* estimate is that the population of the planet will double in one hundred years from 6 billion to *12 billion* people. If the population triples, then we will have *18 billion* or more people on earth. If it quadruples, then our children and grandchildren must survive on this planet with *24 billion* people! And we were only talking about the number for *this* century! The people of the very next century (the twenty-second century) must face populations of at least 24 billion people on this "small" spacecraft called "Earth." If we humans continue operating as we have from the beginning, by the end of the next century (2200), the earth's populations could reach 24 billion to 48 billion people on the planet.

- Can the planet sustain even 12 billion people? Could it sustain 24 to 48 billion?
- Will there be enough air, especially clean air, to breathe?
- Will there be enough water, especially clean water, to drink?
- Will there be enough food, especially good food, to eat?
- Will there be enough clothes, especially warm clothes, to wear?
- Will there be enough homes, especially decent homes, to inhabit?
- Will there be enough medicine, especially basic medicine, to share?
- Will there be enough safety, especially real safety, to coexist?

The simple math, the sheer numbers tell us we have coming toward us a growing global crisis of epic and epidemic proportion. When people cannot find enough clean air to breathe, clean water to drink, decent food to eat, warm clothes to wear, basic medicine to stop the pain, decent shelter in which to stay, or a safe place to protect their families, they become desperate people. Desperate people do desperate things. Anarchy will reign!

In some places, according to Robert D. Kaplan, anarchy already exists or is perilously close. After two years of world research and travel, Kaplan wrote *The Ends of Earth, A Journey to the Frontiers of Anarchy* (Random House, New York, 1996). He described places at or near the state of anarchy: West Africa, Nile Valley, Middle East, Central Asia, and Indochina.

So many of us have been guilty of making fun of those who have called our attention to global issues, such as global warming, destruction of the ozone layer, increased air pollution, strip mining, deforestation, world hunger, global AIDS, and medical mutations. "Alarmists," they have been called.

However, it is time that strategic leaders begin to seriously focus their leadership skills on the growing global crisis. Executives must face not just the survival of their business, but also the survival of their planet.

For life, as we know it, to survive on our planet for another one hundred, two hundred, five hundred, and one thousand years into the next millennium will require strategic global policies, priorities, protocols, procedures, and practices like none the world has ever known.

In the 1500s, the leaders who thought "strategically" thought basically about the health and safety of their families; in the 1600s about their towns; in the 1700s about their states; in the 1800s about their regions; in the 1900s about their countries. This century we must think strategically about our world, our planet, our globe. We must start thinking realistically and strategically about our relatively small, delicate spacecraft, orbiting a small star, in a small galaxy in a massive universe.

What does this have to do with healthcare? Everything!

The population in impoverished parts of the world is growing twice as fast as the rest of the world (Kaplan, p.11). Of the 15 million people with AIDS worldwide, 10 million are in Africa (Kaplan, p.18). *Thirty percent of the earth's inhabitants have **no** access to any healthcare whatsoever.* Fifty percent have no toilets or electricity. Ninety percent of all births occur in the poorest countries on the planet, and one out of five people in the world are infected with the tuberculosis bacterium (Kaplan, p.434-435).

The survival needs of the planet are seven: air, water, food, clothes, shelter, medicine, and safety. Every one of these needs affects the health of individuals and societies. Polluted air, drought-stricken land, contaminated water, malnutrition, starvation, exposure, little or no medicine, excessive pain, and uncontrolled violence breed war, anarchy, chaos, disease, epidemics, and death.

Local, regional, national, and global healthcare policies and practices call for strategies that reduce consumption, pollution, malnutrition, reproduction, and contamination. Moreover, those strategies must include how to redistribute water, food, clothing, medicine, shelter, and safety to communities and continents that desperately need them.

❧

CHAPTER TWENTY-ONE

GLOBAL WARNINGS

Global warnings are also driving us to a new paradigm in healthcare—a healthcare revolution!

What are some of these global warnings?

1. **Population overload.**
2. **Super-diseases.**
3. **Global epidemics.**
4. **Increasingly contaminated air supply.**
5. **Increasingly contaminated and depleted water supply.**
6. **Global deforestation.** Increasing deforestation of our globe is creating a thinning of oxygen, the ozone layer, and increasing amounts of carbon dioxide, carbon monoxide, and ultraviolet radiation. The increasing problem of air pollution, especially in major metropolitan areas, is a major health hazard and a growing one.
7. **Nuclear proliferation.** There is increasing concern regarding the number of countries that now have nuclear weapons and especially that terrorist groups have access to or are capable of manufacturing nuclear weapons. Of greater concern is the nuclear "dirty bomb," which is radioactive nuclear waste attached

to a conventional bomb, creating a cloud of radioactive dust.

8. **Biochemical weapons**. More significantly and obviously very much on the minds of Americans is the manufacture of biochemical weapons. They are easily produced. They can be produced in mass quantities. They can be transported and delivered to large population centers relatively easy. They can have a devastating impact. The anthrax attack has clearly heightened our awareness of the major threat of bioterrorism and of biochemical weapons. We have been warned about them for ninety years. Our oceans will no longer protect us.

9. **World hunger**. Seventy percent of the world goes to bed hungry at night. Thirty percent of the world is experiencing severe levels of malnutrition. The problem of world hunger is escalating. In our culture, the increasing number of people that are overweight or obese is growing while the rest of the world is starving and hungry. Plus, we throw away billions of pounds of food every day.

10. **Global warming**. Different people have different opinions on whether the globe is actually warming or not. If it is, the rise of just two or three feet in the ocean levels would dramatically affect population centers on coastlines around the globe.

11. **Desert expansion**. Desert expansion is another one of the global warnings. It is most prevalent in North Africa, but other sections of the world are seeing their climates become more arid and the amount of desert and arid land is increasing around the globe. This trend cuts into the amount of clean air, clean water, and food that is available.

12. **Soil erosion**. As trees are cut from the land and soil is blown from the land or washed off, this depletes

the quality of the soil. The food grown on this type of soil is more difficult to grow and is less nutritional. There is already a problem in this country, as well. Farmers have used lands for decades, depleting the soil. Trace nutrients are declining in the foods that we buy.

13. **Political instability**. Around the globe the number of unstable countries and economies is growing. The disparity between the haves and the have-nots within communities or between nations breeds violence and chaos, war and suffering, death and disease. Healthcare becomes a casualty.

14. **Global terrorism**. Psychologists and mental health professionals are concerned about the growing number of children without parents or a healthy community in which to live. We know that children without parents, who have not bonded with an adult, develop attachment disorders. They become "kids without a conscience." They are easily drawn into organizations that promote aggression, violence, and terror. Healthcare becomes a hostage and a victim.

If there is any doubt, the difference between 1901 and 2001 is that America no longer lives in an isolated part of the world. It is no longer protected by oceans. It is no longer even protected by massive military superiority. We are not a protected fortress. We are not an isolated island. We are part of a global community impacted by what goes on around the globe. There are warnings coming from around the globe of concerns that the adults and children of this century, even of this decade, must address. These warnings are raising questions that are driving us to new paradigms, including healthcare.

PART TWO

THE ALTERNATIVES: PARTICIPANT-DIRECTED HEALTHCARE

CHAPTER TWENTY-TWO

&

PARTICIPANT-DIRECTED HEALTHCARE

Given all the forces driving the healthcare revolution, what will be the next and new paradigm? Five alternatives are emerging, but they can all be classified as participant-directed healthcare.

From 1910 to 1940, healthcare was often provided directly by the employer who purchased the healthcare. Frequently, the company provided a hospital or pharmacist, a company doctor or company clinic. Therefore, it was *purchaser-provided* and *purchaser-controlled*. Companies started getting out of the business of providing healthcare directly in the late 1930s as community hospitals were formed and doctors became an increasingly independent profession.

From 1940 to 1970, enhanced by the Hill-Burton Act, healthcare was purchased by the employer or the federal government and provided by local physicians and local hospitals. A claim was generated by the providers and sent to the claims administrator, who in turn paid the claim—generally in full. This was especially true in the early stages of the insurance industry. Healthcare in that thirty-year period was *plan-driven,* but in many ways *provider-controlled.*

From 1970 to 2000, healthcare has been controlled by the payor—better known as "managed care." It has been *plan-driven* and *payor-controlled*. The provider, the patient, and even the purchaser of healthcare (the company) had little control over who was seen by whom, when, and how much was paid directly to the provider. Contact was made with a third-party administrator or insurance carrier and the plan design determined what was paid, how much, and when.

Thus, for the last sixty to ninety years, patients have had less and less say about the treatment of their illness and have been given little or no incentive to remain healthy. They have sick days, but lose them if they don't use them. They have sick care benefits, but lose them if they don't use them. Even with a flexible spending account with money set aside, if they don't use it, they lose it. Medical coverage has been provided, but it covers less and less, with more and more restrictions, and more and more hassles for providers and patients. Moreover, employers—that is, the purchasers of healthcare—who want to provide an employee benefit find themselves encumbered by legal liabilities and an ever-increasing entitlement mentality. Employers are being driven out of providing healthcare altogether. As a result, a revolution has begun.

For over thirty years, I have been a participant in this changing paradigm. My involvement in healthcare began in my sophomore year in college when I was taking simultaneously one course in social psychology and another in anatomy and physiology. I loved and enjoyed both courses, made excellent grades, and had a choice of majoring in psychology or in pre-med. For reasons too complicated to explain, I chose psychology with an emphasis in counseling, but I've always remained interested in medicine.

In December of 1970, I became a participant in the healthcare system. While inspecting a new building, I jumped off the last step of a non-skid safety ladder. My college ring got caught and it peeled the flesh off the right ring finger, leaving the ring and crumpled flesh lying in my hand. Like a knife, it "de-gloved" the finger. I was rushed to the hospital and remained in the emergency room for several hours while doctors considered the options. A plastic surgeon, in consultation with an orthopedic surgeon, told me that they planned to save my finger. I had no idea what lay ahead. They didn't even discuss with me all that would be involved in the effort to save that finger. Instead, they performed surgery. They sliced open my chest, attached the bone of what remained of my right ring finger to the skin of my chest. It was called a pectoral graft.

For the next four weeks I remained on the orthopedic surgical wing of the local Medical Center. Every few days they detached a portion of that graft from my chest, forcing the blood supply and nutrients to flow through the skin to nourish the graft. Each day I received shots of Demerol to ease the pain and at night I received one final shot to relax and go to sleep. Each jerk of my arm jerked the hand and all the grafts associated with it.

I remember that at least three roommates came and went during those four weeks. One was involved in a terrible motorcycle accident, another was involved in a car wreck, and another had corrective surgery on his knee. They came in bad shape, got better and went home. Instead, I had four surgeries during that next four-week period, slowly detaching the chest skin and attaching it to the finger so that the graft would take. Finally, on the day before Christmas, the graft was completely detached from my chest and I was released from the hospital.

Before that surgery I was not told what the doctors were about to do to me. Instead, they just cut. During that final surgery, they took skin grafts from my side and placed them over the open cavity of my chest. Then they took skin grafts from my hip to replace the skin grafts from my side. I was in more pain after leaving the hospital than when I entered the emergency room. My chest, side, and leg were left scarred and disfigured. Infection set in and the odor of infected bandages increased while the pain of those skin grafts accelerated.

Two weeks later I went to the plastic surgeon, who had been a plastic surgeon in World War II. My wounds were very minor compared to what he had seen in the war. There was no empathy or sympathy for pain or suffering. Without giving me any pain medication, he ripped off the gauze from my inflamed skin grafts. I now have a *small* sense of what burn victims must endure. The pain is excruciating.

In January of 1971, I returned to college. Because the blood supply flowed through the skin, I had to keep my hand inside my coat, bandaged to keep it warm and to keep the blood flowing. At that time I was student body president and I received a good bit of kidding about acting like Napoleon—walking around with my right hand inside my coat. Because my finger did look like a frankfurter, I was often jokingly offered a bun along with mustard and ketchup for my "hot dog."

Every few weeks I had to fly from Lexington to Columbus for surgery. The plastic surgeon and orthopedic surgeon made continuous attempts to make it look like a finger. One surgery was designed to cut what appeared to be a cuticle in order to insert an artificial fingernail.

Over the next eight years, from 1970 to 1978, I had at least ten operations on my hand. I had very little or no feeling in the skin, so I would constantly cut it. It would bleed and I would not know it until drops of blood fell on my clothes, papers, and books or on the floor, tables, or chairs. It was especially embarrassing to smear blood on the hand, clothes, or furniture of others. When it was cold, because the blood flowed through the skin, the finger would turn blue. I would burn it and wouldn't know it. I would cut it and not feel it. I would jam it and not sense it.

In 1978 I read an article about a new specialty called hand surgery. The story was about an operation on a baseball player who had jumped up while walking down a street to slap a sign and his hand had caught and de-gloved his finger. The article was about the surgery that had been done for that baseball player.

Obviously intrigued, I asked one of our local physicians—Dr. Don Drury—about it. After some research, Don informed me that there were three hand surgeons—one at the University of Florida in Gainesville, the another at Emory University in Atlanta, and a third one at a place called The Hughston Clinic in Columbus, Georgia. I told him that was home for me, and knew all about The Hughston Clinic, and actually knew Dr. Jack Hughston. He came back with the name of Dr. James Andrews.

I tried on several occasions to call Dr. Andrews. Each time, the nurse would ask if I was a patient, and when I answered "no," she said she would have him call me back—and of course, he never did. One day I called a friend—Dr. Ben Moye—at his office, and when I asked for Ben, they put me right through to him. Suddenly I had an idea. The next time I called The Hughston Clinic I asked for "Jim," and in a moment, a voice came through on the other end of the line. He said, "This is Dr. Andrews." I said, "Dr. Andrews, you don't know me. My name is Wayne Anthony. I had a hand injury and I'd like to talk to you about hand surgery."

Dr. Andrews asked me where I was located. I told him Valdosta, Georgia. He asked me where the accident occurred and I told him, "In Columbus, Georgia." He asked, "What year?" I said, "December 1970." Then he said, "Oh yes, I know, you were in room 635." And in stunned disbelief, I asked, "How did you know?" He said that he was a resident when I came in that afternoon. He knew then all about hand surgery and knew what was ahead for me and how easily it would have been to correct the problem and make the hand very functional. Then he said, "But I was just a resident."

What I heard between the lines was that he had recommended hand surgery, but had been ignored by the other two senior physicians. So he said to me, "Come to Columbus, and we'll operate on your hand and within six weeks you will be playing football again."

Sure enough, the surgery lasted less than an hour and within three weeks I could shake hands again and in three more weeks, I was out playing football on Sunday afternoon. I've had little or no problem since then—only occasionally do I feel the "ghost finger" or the "old finger itches," obviously impossible to scratch.

Why tell this lengthy story? First to publicly thank Dr. Jim Andrews. I will always be grateful for his gifted surgery and gracious understanding. Within everyone's lifetime there is or will be a doctor, nurse, or EMT who dramatically touches their life. We need to free them to practice medicine.

Second, the story is told because it represents an era in healthcare. In 1970 no one challenged the doctor even when just experimenting. Explaining medical procedures and outcomes to a patient was not important and not requested. No one seemed worried about the cost—neither the provider, nor the patient, nor the relatives. The delivery system had to change.

In the 1970s patients did not challenge doctors. They could spend thousands for an experiment and no one would challenge their authority to do so. I learned a lot by being a patient for nearly four weeks in a hospital and undergoing fourteen operations to satisfy an experiment, and I learned a lot about the bedside skills of physicians and clergy. I learned what it was like to be an amputee, how it feels when others notice the missing appendage. I certainly understood the pain of skin grafts and the subsequent physical disfigurement that comes with them. I can appreciate what people go through when they have radical breast surgery or massive operations that leave scars and how that impacts the self-image, especially if they are young. Bathing suits and swimming parties become embarrassing events and painful experiences.

In 1974, 1975, and 1978, our three children were born and we watched and experienced the transition that occurred in the way fathers were treated in delivery. But in those days, 100 percent of all our expenses were paid.

In 1979 I began my MBA program at the University of Georgia with an emphasis in strategic planning and human resource management. Part of H.R. was to understand and study benefits and plan designs, to look at the abuse that occurs in healthcare, and to develop plans that would limit the amount of abuse.

During the eight years I worked for R.J.R. Nabisco in operations management, I saw how healthcare costs impacted labor costs, which impacted the bottom line. During the 1970s I also witnessed the transition from defined benefit pension plans to defined contribution pension programs—known as 401ks, 403bs, 457s, and IRAs.

In the 1980s I saw the transition from 100 percent healthcare coverage indemnity plans to various types of managed care plans. In July of 1985, Tyson, our youngest child, was involved in a serious bicycle accident. He hit a brick mailbox, was thrown from his bike and landed chin first in the yard of a neighbor. It shattered his jaw in three places and broke many of his teeth. He was in the hospital for nearly a week with his jaw wired shut. While the physical trauma was enormous, the major medical expenses which exceeded $10,000 were covered. These expenses were paid at 100 percent.

Fifteen years later, my wife Frances Sue went in for surgery. This time she had no choice about which hospital she attended. The services she received were excellent. However, she had no choice. We had to pay a deductible of $1,000. The plan only paid 80 percent of agreed-upon fees for outpatient surgery. Five or ten years earlier she would have been an inpatient for three days. Instead, the plan only approved outpatient surgery. She was in the hospital less than eight hours and dismissed.

From 1979 to 1987, I was involved as a *purchaser* of healthcare. From 1987 to present day, I have been involved as a *provider* of healthcare and a consultant to healthcare. As a Senior Professional in Human Resources (SPHR), I have had the privilege of working with employers on healthcare policy and practices. In 1995, I was invited to chair the employer committee of major companies in Columbus, redesigning healthcare. It was my privilege to represent small employers in an effort to negotiate equitable healthcare plans and providers fees.

In 1996, I became a key contact for the National Legislative Committee of the Society for Human Resource Management (SHRM). In 1998, I was selected as the Georgia State Legislative Director and a consultant to the National Legislative Committee. In 2000, I was invited to serve as a member of the National Legislative Committee of SHRM and lead its focus on healthcare legislation.

Thus, for the last five years, I have been working with the staffs of nearly thirty members of Congress to write healthcare legislation for the new healthcare paradigm. We have worked with both Houses of Congress and both political parties to facilitate the transition from a plan-design, payor-controlled healthcare system to a participant-directed, patient-controlled health and wellness system. In 2003, that transition began.

Participant-directed healthcare has several features. Participants have far more control over the plan in which they participate, the providers they choose, and the services they receive. They are rewarded financially for staying healthy and living healthier lifestyles. Individuals, organizations, or governments make *defined contributions* to the plans, similar to 401k plans. In fact, they are often called "401h plans." And a special feature of three of the defined contribution healthcare plans is that unused healthcare dollars can roll over to successive years. Hence no longer will people lose it if they don't use it. If they stay healthy, their healthcare funds actually accumulate with interest. Participants choose their own providers. Providers are rewarded for providing good patient care and quality service at a reasonable cost.

Defined contribution healthcare takes five different forms or arrangements, which we will examine in the following chapters.

CHAPTER TWENTY-THREE

DEFINED CONTRIBUTION: CASH SYSTEM

With a defined contribution cash system, employers get out of the business of healthcare altogether. They give their employees a certain amount of money, a defined contribution, and then employees are instructed to go buy healthcare or health insurance. If employees use it for anything other than healthcare and insurance, it is treated as taxable income, so they are encouraged to buy health insurance.

There is precedent for this. In the early 1900s, employers provided almost all the services and needs of employees. They provided housing, utilities, transportation, recreation, education, clothes, healthcare, medicine, even a general store where employees and their families could buy food and clothes. Over time, because of different factors, employers quit providing all those goods and services. Instead, they paid employees more, allowing the employees to purchase their own housing, provide their own utilities, purchase their own transportation, seek out their own recreation, and purchase their own clothes. While employers may have assisted communities in building schools, they no longer actually provided the schools. Now employers give employees the money and let them buy their own entertainment and transportation.

Housing was one of the most difficult things for companies to provide, because people complained of discrimination. Yet, because it was so expensive, housing was difficult for employees to provide for themselves. It was a huge purchase— even in the 1920s and 1930s. There was great debate over whether employees could make such big decisions for themselves. What if they made a mistake purchasing their homes and squandered their life savings?

The collapse of the stock market, the Great Depression, and World War II changed much of the paternalistic thinking of companies. G.I.s went to war and then returned. They received G.I. benefits for education and V.A. loans for housing.

Healthcare, however, has remained the last vestige of the company store. But it, too, is going through the same transition. Employers can no longer please all the employees and their relatives with the current illness treatment system. Healthcare benefits were established during the wage freeze of World War II. It was a way of attracting and keeping good employees. But in more recent years it has become a significant source of complaints and in the last five years, a source of potential legal as well as monetary liability. So employers are thinking more and more about giving employees the money and letting them buy their own healthcare and then live with their decisions.

From 1935 to 1970 the government, as well as companies, promised employees "We'll take care of you." The government said, "If you contribute to Social Security, when you get ready to retire, your pension program will be funded and the government will take care of you in your old age." Employers said, "If you remain loyal to the company, when you retire, we will pay you for the years you worked for us" (the old defined-benefit pension programs). So employees spent their lifetime working for one company and contributed every payday to Social Security (FICA). They accumulated years of service with an expectation that when they retired, the company would pay them increasing amounts based on the number of years they served the company.

Starting in the 1970s, things began to change. Concerns over the Social Security Trust Fund and its financial viability have caused great debate. What will America do when all the Baby Boomers hit retirement? Moreover, the decline and fall of major companies has shattered the old myths about company pension programs and employee loyalty. Enron and Worldcom are two of the biggest disasters to hit in years.

Companies can no longer promise long-term, lifetime employment. The fact is people are being laid off. Business and government were pressured to create defined contribution pension programs where employees could contribute, often more than the company could afford to contribute, and thus increase their retirement benefits. Again, healthcare is going through that same transition now. Give employees the money and let them buy their own

The advantage of the cash system is that the employees have total control of their money. The employer is out of it—no liability, no risk; the employee bears all of the risk. Hence, the major disadvantage of cash-based, defined contribution healthcare plans is that employees with limited healthcare education might make poor decisions about their healthcare dollar, or misuse their dollar and spend it on things other than healthcare. Then when they need it, they have no money available for healthcare and go into debt. Meanwhile, employers need healthy workers who might go elsewhere to work for a company that provides healthcare benefits.

Another great disadvantage of the cash system is buying power. The individual employee looking for healthcare is subject to the cost of single coverage rates and has little negotiating power with a limited amount of healthcare education. If things don't go well, they have no one to advocate for them, either with the provider or with the payor. So, defined contribution cash plans have been met with very little enthusiasm.

If the other four options do not work, expect companies to give their employees cash to buy their own coverage in five to ten years.

Chapter Twenty-Four

Defined Contribution: Voucher System

Under the voucher system, the employer negotiates with insurers and then recommends several reputable insurance carriers to their employees. Employees may then choose which insurer and which plan they prefer. The employer provides a fixed amount made available for the purpose of purchasing insurance. In that sense, it's a defined contribution. They give the employee a voucher that says, "This is how much you have available to purchase healthcare," and then the employee negotiates directly with insurance carriers that have been recommended. Once they've selected an insurance company and plan, the insurance carrier bills the employer and the employer pays the carrier.

In the process of choosing a carrier and plan design, the employee may select a plan that costs more than the company voucher will cover. In that case, the employee must pay the difference for the coverage. Employees may pay it directly by writing a check or have the amount automatically withdrawn from their paycheck through payroll deduction. The company sends the amount directly to the insurer. The employer contribution is a tax-deductible expense and the employee contribution is paid with pre-tax dollars. Most employees prefer to have it taken out by payroll deduction, and most insurers, to make sure that they get the payment, would prefer the payment be handled by the company.

The value of a defined contribution voucher system for the employer is that it creates a fixed expense. It also allows employers to treat all employers the same. It doesn't matter whether the employee is young, old, single, married, has a domestic partner, is married with children or single with children, or has a spouse covered by another plan. The amount that the company pays is based strictly on the employee. Another advantage to the employer is that their employees have good insurance coverage through a reputable, recommended insurer.

One of the big advantages for employees is that employers can negotiate discounts because they represent a larger group. Another advantage for employees is the value of having the company advocate for them. Equally important is the fact that all employees are treated the same—fairly—regardless of their marital situation, age, economic situation, position in the company, etc.

There are some disadvantages. The employer may have limited influence on the carrier the employee ultimately chooses. Employees may choose the cheapest available healthcare option. The employee loses some of the advantage of group discounts. Both employers and employees are subject to whatever insurance carriers are willing to offer and the advantages of steerage and group participation is lost.

Other disadvantages include the continuing focus on illness treatment and very little reward for healthy lifestyles. It is still a plan-driven, payor-controlled system. Employees either use health coverage or they lose it. If you remain healthy you only have protection if you need healthcare (term illness insurance). If you are sick and need healthcare reimbursement, you have it based on the policy you have chosen.

Perhaps the greatest disadvantage is that many employees will opt for the cheapest coverage available instead of the most appropriate coverage. Plus, there is still no reward for wellness. There is no incentive to be a wise healthcare consumer. Big employers will still get big discounts. Small employers and self-employed people are left with expensive coverage. Costs are subject to the rate experience of the group of people covered. Those who anticipate needing healthcare costs will opt for that which covers their needs the best. This "adverse selection" will drive up healthcare beyond affordability or drive insurers away. The healthy employees opt out of the more expensive plans, making those plans even more expensive.

Co-payments or co-insurance are paid by the employee, the patient. The insurer negotiates with providers and they agree upon rates to be reimbursed. Out-of-network providers may balance-bill—that is charge patients the difference between in-network and out-of-network charges.

Because of all the disadvantages of the voucher system, few employees, legislators, benefit managers, or human resource professionals are seriously considering or recommending it. Employers and unions are not advocates of this system either.

CHAPTER TWENTY-FIVE

DEFINED CONTRIBUTION: SPENDING ACCOUNTS

Several interrelated phrases are being used for defined contribution spending accounts (Personal Care Accounts, Healthcare Spending Accounts, Medical Spending Accounts, as well as Flexible Spending Accounts). Basically they are all accounts into which an employer contributes a defined amount each year. The allocated funds can only be used for health-related expenses.

Under the new arrangements, "defined contribution spending accounts," employers would set aside a fixed amount each year for each employee to use to pay IRS-approved medical or health expenses. The employee never has "constructive receipt" of these funds. They do not "own" this money. The company still "owns" the money, but it has been allocated and set aside for each employee in a medical spending account.

For example, a company may allocate $3,000 per year for each employee. The employee may be reimbursed from that medical spending account for any health-related expense incurred. When the $3,000 is used up the employee must pay the next $3,000 "out of pocket" from his own funds. The company may then have a major medical catastrophic policy that "kicks in" after the company's $3,000 and the employee's $3,000 have both been used.

There are obviously variations on the amount the employer may choose to allocate for each employee and how much the employee must pay before major medical kicks in.

What's more, the amount being set aside each year by the employer for each employee, if unused, can be rolled over to the next year.

For example, if the employer sets aside $3,000 each year for an employee in a medical spending account and the employee only uses $1,000, then the remaining $2,000 is "rolled over" to the following year. The next year the employer sets aside another $3,000 per employee. Now the employee has $5,000 for healthcare before having to use a single penny of his own money.

As long as the employee and his dependents stay healthy, the medical spending account balance increases. Again, the funds can only be used to reimburse healthcare related expenses.

In this case, the employer sets aside a fixed amount per employee. The employer solicits insurance carriers to offer major medical plans to her employees; or the employer may select a plan for her employees; or the employer may self-fund major medical using a third-party administrator to negotiate preferred provider arrangements. The employee chooses which plan option she wants and uses some of the defined contribution to pay for it.

The employee chooses which provider he wants and the services he wants to receive. The employee (patient) may choose to go in-network. If so, the plan will pay 80 percent of agreed-upon rates and the employee pays 20 percent. The employee (patient) may go out-of-network. Then the plan still pays 80 percent of the in-network rate, but the employee (patient) and provider must negotiate on the balance remaining. The employee (patient) pays the provider and then gets reimbursed. The in-network rate is a pre-negotiated rate. The final out-of-network rate is negotiated by the patient. The plan only reimburses the employee at the in-network percentage rate. The employee must pay the balance with his own money.

There are some unique advantages to this system. There is a set amount paid by the employer and it is the same whether the person is single, married, with family, without family, has a domestic partner, etc. The employee then chooses which plan, which provider, and which services she wants and then is reimbursed for the healthcare using the employer's dollars first. Employers would contribute a certain amount each year with a certain inflation factor attached to annual increases.

There is another advantage in this type of arrangement. There is no deductible as such. The patient (employee) has a financial stake in every healthcare decision. She can spend the "set aside" amount on staying healthy and roll more and more money into her medical spending account year after year. Or she can use it up being sick. Thus, there is a big incentive to stay well.

The advantage to the employer is the fixed expense. It is a defined contribution that covers basic healthcare. There is a strong financial incentive to employees to stay healthy. The employee still has the employer to help negotiate, recommend, promote, and advocate among quality healthcare providers. Every employee has basic healthcare and major medical coverage.

There are disadvantages. Certainly the employees are still exposed to overall healthcare increases. Moreover, someone's poor lifestyle behavior could create a catastrophic healthcare claim that would then impact the whole group.

There is the risk that employees will still not make good healthcare choices. They may not take advantage of annual physicals or participate in weight management or health promotion programs. They may spend their healthcare allotments on unnecessary health care services or healthcare products. Or they may delay illness treatment until it becomes acute and expensive.

Many employees and their dependents will have a difficult time negotiating with their physician or questioning the recommendations of a doctor. They may be reluctant to get and pay for a second opinion. In essence, will employees be good informed careful consumers of healthcare?

Another major concern is older employees or chronically ill employees (or their dependents). Their treatment needs are greater and more expensive. They will quickly use up the company allocation and have to spend their own money. Accumulating money in a medical spending account may be an impossibility.

Still another disadvantage from the employee's perspective is that this account is not portable. If they leave the company, they leave the money. That is, she leaves the amount that's been accumulated in her name. Under current law the company still "owns" the money. The employee does not have "constructive receipt" or ownership of the money. The truth is, the employee never owned it in the first place; it was not a part of her salary. It was a benefit set aside for her while she was an employee (like free access to the company fitness center). So if the employee leaves, she leaves it behind.

A final disadvantage is that, under current law, these funds may not be protected should the company be sold, get into financial difficulty, or declare bankruptcy.

In spite of the disadvantages, employers have or are seriously considering this option. What employers like most about it is that it's a fixed amount per employee and, for the first time, it financially encourages people to be healthy and be proactive, informed, and conscientious healthcare consumers.

Chapter Twenty-Six

ॐ

Defined Contribution: Savings Accounts

The opening session of the Health Agenda 2002 Conference in Washington, D.C., on March 7, 2002, was entitled *"From 401(k) to 401 (h): Toward Employee-Driven Health Benefits."* Four people representing some of the largest and most innovative entities in the healthcare industry presented the case for the transition to employee-driven healthcare: Brian Marcotte, Vice President, Benefits and Compensation, Honeywell; Robert O'Brien, Jr., Worldwide Partner, William M. Mercer, Inc.; Pamela Krol, Director, Health and Welfare Programs, Lucent Technologies; and Kelly Jenkins, Manager, Health and Life Programs, Federal Express Corporation.

They followed an opening keynote address by Leonard Schaeffer, Chairman and CEO of Wellpoint Health Networks, Inc. The title of his address on March 6, 2002, was *"Twenty-First Century Healthcare: Meeting the Challenge."*

Each speaker echoed seven consistent themes:

1. The cost of healthcare is soaring (up 50 percent in the last five years).
2. The plan-driven, payor-controlled system is no longer working.

3. Employees (patients) must become financial partners in all healthcare decisions.
4. Providers must share financial risks in all treatment decisions.
5. A healthcare system that rewards good health is a necessity.
6. Employers want to help their employees get good healthcare.
7. Corporate America is *quickly* moving toward defined contribution health plans.

The form that defined contribution health plans may take is still unclear because of patient and provider confusion and misunderstanding of the current tax laws, regulations, and restrictions.

The Section 125 flexible spending account allows employees to "set aside" some of their pre-tax wages to pay for uncovered medical expenses. That is, they are reimbursed for out-of-pocket medical expenses. However, if they do not use it, they lose it. Under current law, it cannot be "rolled over" to the next year.

In the current flexible spending account, an employee designates a portion of his pre-tax salary to be allocated to these spending accounts. The money is deducted by the company each pay period before taxes are assessed and deposited in a flexible spending account. When an employee or his dependent incurs a medical expense not covered under his health plan, he can submit the documented receipt for reimbursement up to the maximum annual allocation. If the employee does not use all of the designated funds, he loses them.

The unused funds are returned to the employer's healthcare funding mechanism. The employee never has "constructive receipt" of these designated funds. He cannot spend them any way he wants. He doesn't "own" the money and thus does not have to pay income taxes on it.

The medical spending account described in Chapter Twenty-Five allows an employer to "set aside" money for each employee to use for any medical or healthcare expense up to the limit of the allocated amount (e.g., $3,000). If money still remains in the employee's account at the end of the year, then it can be rolled over to the next year. The employer makes an annual defined contribution to the accounts and the money for healthcare grows.

A weakness in medical spending accounts is the lack of portability. What happens if there is a layoff or the employee must relocate and leave the company? Another weakness is the need for employees to *save* money while they are healthy.

Enter the Healthcare Savings Account! With a Healthcare Savings Account (HSA), employers make a defined cash contribution directly to a healthcare plan on behalf of the employee. This contribution is not considered by the IRS as income and can only be used for healthcare expenditures.

With a few legislative tax changes, the HSA can work to encourage healthy lifestyles and help employees save money for healthcare expenses. The employer makes a defined contribution to the employee's HSA. Employees could also contribute some of their pre-tax dollars to the HSA. The money and interest accumulates tax-deferred. These funds can only be administered by a third-party administrator (TPA) and can only be used to reimburse healthcare expenses.

Employees could and should use some of the money to purchase health (illness) insurance, and the employer could use some of its contribution to purchase major medical coverage for each employee. Participants would pay for medical services or healthcare products with a medical debit card or be reimbursed for those medical expenses. Providers could also send an itemized bill to the patient, and the patient would review and approve all items, sign the invoice, and submit a request for payment to the TPA. The TPA would then pay the provider directly and send a copy to the patient.

There are some compelling advantages to this system. Every employee receives the same defined healthcare contribution. Employers have a fixed expense adjusted annually according to the Consumer Price Index. Employees can and should contribute to this true HSA.

What is most exciting is that the unused healthcare dollars from the employer and employee gain interest tax-free, can only be used for healthcare expenses, are rolled over, and accumulate year after year.

Another advantage to a HSA is that it is issued to *reimburse* many healthcare expenses, thus getting the patient (employee) more involved financially in healthcare decisions. Employees and their dependents become more aware of the cost of healthcare and illness treatment. Employees and their dependents are financially rewarded for being and staying healthy.

A big advantage to a HSA occurs when circumstances force an employee to move or leave the company. She can take her *health* dollars with her and roll them into another plan. The employee is truly rewarded for being a healthy person and is financially rewarded for remaining well and working.

There is an important national benefit for working people, especially when they are young and healthy. They need to build up their HSAs to help them with medical expenses in retirement and old age. Society, Social Security, families, and the Federal Government are going to be overwhelmed by the illness treatment of a huge aging population if we do not allow HSAs.

There is, however, one major weakness. What about self-employed people, employees in small firms, and employees of non-profit organizations? They have little or no leverage to get big discounts on health-related insurance, services, pharmaceuticals, supplies, and products. What about the 31 million uninsured but employed people in America? Even big business recognizes the need to do something for small business, non-profits, and the self-employed. Not only is it the right thing to do, but it's cost-effective, as their medical costs are currently being shifted to big business. Moreover, at-risk or chronic users are adversely selecting or remaining with big companies. Why? For healthcare benefits.

So, what's the solution?

❧

CHAPTER TWENTY-SEVEN

DEFINED-CONTRIBUTION: COMMUNITY/ STATE HEALTHCARE COOPERATIVES

A community or state healthcare cooperative is a healthcare solution in which organizations, individuals, or governments make a defined contribution into a community or state healthcare trust fund. Because it is a community or state healthcare cooperative, everyone, including employees from large, midsize, and small companies as well as self-employed persons, may participate in the same very large community or state healthcare cooperative.

In a community or state healthcare cooperative, everyone from an entire community or state pools their healthcare dollars and collectively purchases healthcare services. The funds are placed in a Voluntary Employee Beneficiary Association (VEBA) trust fund that is deposited in a bank or banks and is governed by specific congressional laws and extensive IRS regulations. Trustees of the fund contract with local or regional providers—directly or through insurance carriers— to provide services for their participants at competitive rates. Participants then choose which provider or services they want and the providers are paid promptly.

Purchasers (individuals, organizations, or governments) make a "defined contribution" to the plan, and employees make up the difference, if any. Participants are rewarded for healthy lifestyles, preventive medicine, and early intervention. Access to healthcare is expanded, hassles with healthcare are minimized, quality of healthcare is valued, and accountability and responsibility for healthy lifestyles are expected.

A Voluntary Employee Beneficiary Association (VEBA) was established in the Employee Retirement Income Security Act of 1974 (ERISA). Over the years it has been refined by various IRS regulations and tax reform acts, making it a tried and tested body of legislation and regulation. Moreover, it has broad acceptance and support from both political parties, business and labor organizations, government agencies, and professional entities.

With a minor change in the law, communities or states across the country may establish a tax-exempt trust fund to reimburse participants and providers for life, sickness, accident, and wellness benefits. The contribution to the VEBA is tax deductible.

Benefits paid to providers or reimbursed to participants are not taxable as long as they are used for sickness, accident, life insurance, or wellness benefits. Permissible benefits include burial benefits, payable by reason of death or paid by the Trust for the purchase of life insurance. The IRS also allows for the payment of sick and accident benefits furnished to or on behalf of the member or member's dependent in the event of illness or personal injury. Benefits allowed include amounts paid to a member in lieu of income during a period in which the member cannot work because of sickness or injury, or benefits designed to safeguard and improve the health of a member and his dependents.

The Trust can pay benefits directly to a provider or through reimbursement to a participant or a member's dependents or to an insurance company, medical clinic, or other healthcare provider. It also allows for other benefits, including the paying of wellness benefits or reimbursing wellness facilities or subsidizing wellness activities and wellness education benefits.

Congress needs to make two small changes in the existing ERISA law. First, anyone in the same geographical area should be able to participate. Second, Healthcare Savings Accounts should be available to everyone, contributions should increase tax-deferred, rollover each year, and be portable.

The advantages of a community healthcare cooperative are enormous. Organizations could make a defined contribution and know that their healthcare expenses are fixed. The threat of lawsuits and the unnecessary high cost of liability insurance would be reduced.

Participants are put in the driver's seat of their own healthcare. They are given choices about providers and services, given responsibility and accountability for their health and healthcare. They are rewarded for maintaining their health and pursuing healthy lifestyles. They are rewarded for seeking healthcare education and taking a participative role with providers and services.

Another advantage of a community or state healthcare cooperative is peer pressure. Participants benefit if people stay well and live healthy lifestyles. The community or state benefits if people live right and stay healthy. The community or state also benefits in other ways. People from large and small organizations as well as the self-employed, the uninsured worker, Medicare and Medicaid participants all have access to affordable, quality healthcare. Participants from large organizations benefit from an even larger pool of participants. The costs of benefits are reduced, the impact of large cases is not as great, and adverse selection is eliminated.

Providers benefit because they are both participants in plan design and participants in the health plans themselves. They are providing healthcare to themselves and their own dependents, friends, neighbors, and relatives. All entities, regardless of size, are able to get healthcare coverage for their participants at a reasonable rate.

Because one-third of all healthcare dollars are spent on the overmanagement of healthcare, this should dramatically decrease paperwork, administrative hassles, and the cost of providing healthcare services. This should mean that participants get prompt, appropriate services, while providers get prompt, appropriate reimbursement, and purchasers get reasonable rates and participant satisfaction. It should substantially reduce excessive litigation, because participants make the decision. They now have choices about what they receive and from whom they receive it.

There are very few, if any, disadvantages to a community healthcare cooperative. Employees are rewarded for healthy lifestyles but also suffer from unhealthy lifestyle choices. They will be held responsible and accountable for their healthcare and the healthcare of their dependents. Employees (patients) will face some tough choices, especially with regard to high-risk, experimental, elective, or expensive treatments, products, procedures, and services. Patients will also be faced with some tough choices about catastrophic, terminal illnesses and the amount of futile treatment they will seek. Patients will always have some financial exposure in the choices they make. Providers will also have financial exposure in all decisions and hence not be rewarded for excessive medical treatment and medical experimentation.

Congress needs to provide three clarifications to the current VEBA legislation. First, it needs to enable anyone in the same geographical area to join the VEBA rather than only employees "engaged in the same line of business." Second, Congress needs to clarify the use of VEBA funds for non-taxable wellness benefits when provided by qualified 501(C)(3) healthcare organizations. Third, Congress needs to make Healthcare Saving Accounts (HSA) available to anyone with provisions for employer and employee contributions, rollover, and portability.

These clarifications fall within the original intent or objective of the congressional legislation. Currently, only employees working for employers "engaged in the *same* line of business" within the same geographical area can form a VEBA. The original intent of the legislation was to allow employees from ten or more small employers to collectively form a healthcare trust in order to purchase healthcare on a more competitive basis. But because of the restrictions embodied in the phrase "same line of business," small businesses have been unable to form such healthcare trusts.

Instead, VEBAs have been used extensively and very successfully by large and mid-size employers. The proposed legislation would make it possible for everyone in the same state to participate in the State Healthcare Trust and collectively purchase healthcare services including wellness, sickness, and accident benefits. The legislation would thus benefit employees in any size organization. It would especially benefit employees and their families in small businesses who cannot access large group discounts or who are not covered at all because their small company cannot afford benefits for employees. The healthcare cooperative would also benefit all employers, enabling them to make a defined contribution to these plans, thus stabilizing healthcare costs to an annual cost of living rate increase.

The legislation has the added advantage of putting participants in a position of designing the benefit plan while at the same time having fiduciary responsibility for the financial solvency and stability of the Trust. Providers benefit because plan designs, patients, and reimbursements are no longer controlled by large, out-of-state, profit-making managed-care corporations, but instead are actually managed by people who live and work with them and use and pay for the services. Providers, purchasers, patients, relatives, local politicians and regulators all actually participate in the same community healthcare cooperative. It puts purchasers of healthcare, participants in healthcare, and providers of healthcare back in charge of healthcare and its delivery system.

Equally important, the community or state healthcare cooperative encourages, reimburses, and rewards wellness and prevention. Thus, the community or state healthcare cooperative could dramatically improve the way healthcare is delivered, simplify how it is paid, and include all Americans who are unable to buy affordable healthcare coverage.

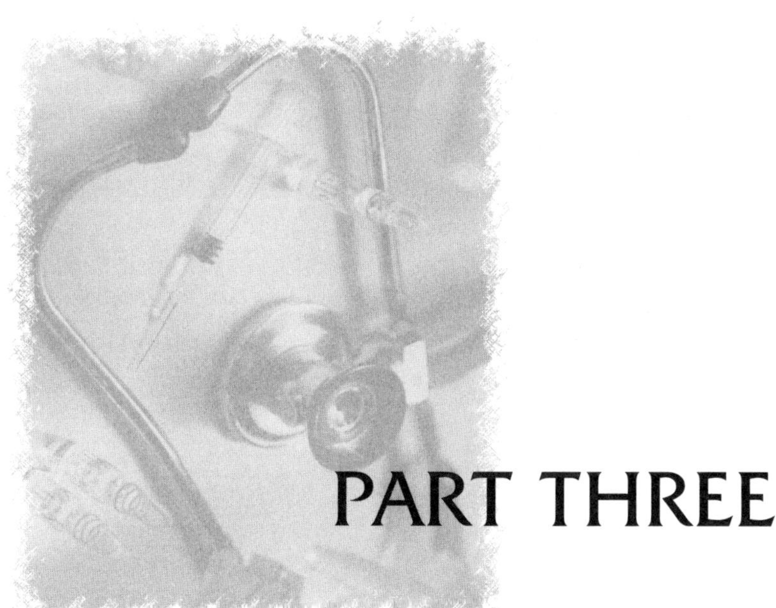

PART THREE

THE SOLUTION: COMMUNITY/STATE HEALTHCARE COOPERATIVES

&

Chapter Twenty-Eight

Introduction: The Healthcare Solution

The most significant change in healthcare in the last sixty years has begun. Over the last five years, strategic planners in healthcare have been predicting a transition from a **plan-driven** healthcare system to a **participant-directed** healthcare system.

Healthcare is moving from a payor-controlled system to a participant-controlled system in which participants select physicians, specialists, treatment, and services. Moreover, organizations, individuals, or governments make "defined contributions" to those healthcare plans. Participants make up the difference based on their choice of provider and services.

Several names have been used to refer to this new system—patient-directed healthcare system, consumer-driven healthcare, or defined contribution health plans.

On December 10, 2001, *The Wall Street Journal* carried an article that brought the issue to front and center in the healthcare debate. The article, "Employers expect healthcare costs to rise 14 percent in 2002," was written by Barbara Martinez, staff reporter. In the article, Martinez says, "The picture for the health insurance costs keeps getting uglier for employers and consumers alike." Employers experienced a 14 percent rise in 2002 and a 22 percent increase in 2003.

Some companies were hit with increases of 20 percent or more, according to a survey released by William M. Mercer, Inc., a human resource consulting firm.

The Mercer survey of more than 2,800 employers estimated that the average cost to companies for each employee rose 11.2 percent to $4,924 in 2001. It is the largest increase in nine years and grew at a rate three times that of inflation. The double-digit healthcare cost came as a weakened economy hit individuals, families, and organizations. Moreover, aging Baby Boomers will require more medical attention and prescription drugs over the next decade even as healthcare plans restrict access and require higher co-payments.

Martinez went on to indicate an even more alarming number. "According to recent government projections, healthcare spending in the U.S. is expected to double over the next decade to $2.6 trillion." In response, 40 percent of large employers said they will require employees to pay a higher percentage of the cost next year. According to Blaine Dubois, a Mercer principal, companies are looking for at least four more years of double-digit inflation.

So, what are employers planning to do? In addition to passing the cost on to employees, according to Martinez, "more and more employers are offering their employees defined contribution health plans in which employees manage their own healthcare dollars. These accounts offer incentives for members to choose generic over name-brand drugs and encourage them to shop around for doctors and medical services." According to the Mercer survey, 29 percent of the employers with more than 20,000 workers said they were "somewhat" or "very likely" to adopt such an approach within the next two years.

What's driving this rapid transition to patient-controlled healthcare plans? A number of factors have already been listed: The rising cost of healthcare and the aging workforce, including Baby Boomers and their insatiable demand for all types of medical services.

In addition, a number of factors are forcing employers to get out of the healthcare business, among them the Patient's Bill of Rights, the threat of lawsuits, the armada of attorneys connected with REPAIR, and jury awards of over $100 million dollars where plans have restricted access to services. All of these are pushing employers, and will eventually push government to reconsider healthcare plans that in any way direct or restrict access to healthcare providers or services.

For the last three years, experts have been anticipating a dramatic shift in healthcare, and in 2001 the revolution came into view. *Psychotherapy Finance*, the leading practice publication for behavioral health providers, ran a cover story in its December 2001 issue entitled "Are We Ready for a Self-Pay World?" The article said, "The ground is shifting, and a growing number of employers are considering a dramatic change, downloading healthcare decisions and cost to employees." It concluded, "Defined contribution health plans are taking off."

Then, in the cover story for the January, 2002, issue of *HR Magazine*, "Containing Growing Healthcare Costs," the lead article proclaimed: "Defined Contribution Coverage is designed to cut costs by giving workers more control over their healthcare sources." The *HR* article continued, "Lacking a magic wand to cure the ills of health coverage, many consultants are laying out what's called the defined-contribution approach, which tries to match consumer choice and cost savings. In defined contribution arrangements, participating employees have choices. For example, in 401(k) pension plans, employees choose from various investment options. In defined contribution health plans, employees choose the medical benefits that best suits their needs. Some companies have already begun such plans in 2002."

Companies using the defined contribution health plan include Radnor Holdings Corporation from Radnor, PA,

Charter Communication Inc., Novartis Corporation, Aetna, Inc., Raytheon Company, Trover Solutions, Inc., Textron, Inc., Kraft Foods, Inc., General Mills, Inc., and Wells Fargo Bank.

Several major insurers are getting involved also: Aetna, Inc. based in Hartford, CT; Humana, Inc. in Louisville, KY; Wellpoint from Thousand Oaks, CA; Lumenos, Inc. of Alexandria, VA; Definity Health Corporation of Minneapolis, MN; and Blue Cross/Blue Shield of Pennsylvania.

For sixty years, healthcare has been controlled by plan designs and managed by payors. The shift to defined contribution health plans means:

- Participants will have greater control, responsibility, and accountability for their own healthcare.
- Providers will have fewer hassles and more input in delivering healthcare.
- Families will have more influence and responsibility for their health.
- People will be rewarded for staying healthy.
- The system will focus on healthcare rather than illness care.

Thus, the solution for many of America's healthcare challenges is the formation of community healthcare cooperatives. Everyone from an entire community or state pools their healthcare dollars into a healthcare trust fund. The trustees of the fund contract with local and regional providers directly or through insurance carriers to provide services for all of their members and dependents at reasonable rates. Patients choose which provider and services they want and the agreed-upon reimbursement would be paid promptly.

Two pieces of legislation are needed from Congress for this to happen.

First, Congress needs to facilitate community or state healthcare cooperatives by allowing community or state healthcare trusts (VEBAs) to include anyone in the same geographical area. This would allow everyone in a community or state to participate in a large healthcare cooperative and reap the same benefits that only large employers now receive. Providers could participate in the same association and the administrative costs of healthcare; inevitable hassles involved would be dramatically cut or eliminated. Hence, more of the healthcare dollars spent by individuals, organizations, or governments would flow directly to those who actually provide the service.

Second, Congress needs to pass legislation allowing anyone to have Healthcare Savings Accounts (HSA). The HSA allows purchasers to make a defined contribution each year to an HSA and deduct it as a standard business expense. It can only be used for health-related purposes. Participants could also contribute pretax dollars to the HSA. Any unused portion would be rolled over to the next year. The funds are contributed to the healthcare trust, and thus "belong" to the participant and can only be used for healthcare.

Chapter Twenty-Nine

Community Healthcare Cooperatives

The structure being recommended is a community-wide or statewide healthcare trust. These trusts were established in the Employee Retirement Income Security Act of 1974 (ERISA) and over the years have been refined by various IRS regulations and tax reform acts. Thus, they are a tried and tested body of legislation and regulation. Moreover, these trusts have broad acceptance and are used by both political parties, business and labor organizations, government agencies, and professional entities.

A community or state healthcare cooperative would give everyone, including those who are self-employed in the same geographical area, access to affordable, quality healthcare. Employers and employees, as well as those self-employed, could collectively purchase affordable healthcare through this IRS-approved healthcare trust. The healthcare trust is directed by elected participants (trustees). Community-based providers work with community-based trust officers to secure healthcare services for community-based participants and their dependents, including the uninsured dependents living with them.

The community or state healthcare cooperative enables organizations, especially small ones, to offer their people affordable, quality healthcare. The Trust then gives participants and their families more choices regarding the services they seek (clinics, hospitals, professional, laboratory, ancillary, pharmaceutical, dental, wellness) and the providers they use. Along with greater choice, people would have greater responsibility and accountability for their lifestyle and healthcare decisions.

The purpose of a healthcare trust, as stated in Section 501(C)(9) of the Internal Revenue Code, is to provide "life, sick, accident, and other benefits intended to safeguard or improve the health of a member...." IRS regulations define a dependent as:

- The spouse of the member
- Any child of the member or the member's spouse
- Any other minor or child residing with the member
- Any other individual considered as a dependent for federal tax purposes

The IRS permits contributions made by an employer to the Trust to be tax-deductible. Contributions made on behalf of participants by an organization are treated as non-taxable income. Participants can make additional contributions to the plan with pretax payroll dollars. Benefits paid by the plan for life, sick, accident, and other approved benefits are non-taxable benefits.

The Internal Revenue Service has been very accommodating in defining non-taxable benefits that can be paid from the VEBA Trust (healthcare plan). Permissible benefits include:

Life Insurance	Medical Benefits
Disability Insurance	Dental Benefits
Wellness Benefits	Illness Benefits

In essence, healthcare-related expenses can be paid from the plan without taxable consequences, meaning income tax-free.

Congress originally designed VEBAs for small businesses and small professional groups to allow ten or more employers in the same line of business in the same geographical area to pool their premiums and collectively purchase healthcare, receiving discounts available only to large employers.

Great idea. Almost worked. One problem.

That problem has been the "same line of business" stipulation, which meant only competitors could meet together, discuss their finances, and pool their healthcare money. However, employers feared being accused of price fixing or collusion.

Thus, the legislation had the effect of limiting the use of this well-known healthcare purchasing mechanism to large businesses and labor unions. Removing an unintended restriction would enable these plans to be used by participants and their families from all organizations regardless of size, including the self-employed. It would also allow participants to include the uninsured and those receiving support from government entities.

It is proposed that the restriction "same line of business" be removed to allow anyone to form a community or state healthcare cooperative.

The community healthcare cooperative is a 501(C)(9) trust fund operated by participants who have been elected as trustees. The Trust contracts with local or regional providers directly or through insurance carriers to provide quality, affordable, community-based healthcare for all its members and their families. It brings the cost and control as well as direction and delivery of healthcare back to the community or state and entrusts it directly to those involved—patients, providers, and purchasers.

❦

CHAPTER THIRTY

WHO BENEFITS?

Providers of healthcare benefit from the community or state healthcare cooperative because the plan design is simple, patients choose providers and services, and reimbursement comes quickly or instantly.

Purchasers of healthcare benefit because their participants have more involvement in design, cost, quality, utilization, and outcomes.

Participants utilizing healthcare benefit because they have more choices of healthcare services and more control of their healthcare decisions. In addition, costs are reasonable when the risk is shared and lifestyle is considered. Best of all, participants are rewarded for making good healthcare decisions and lifestyle choices.

Relatives of members benefit because members know their families are adequately covered, have access to affordable, quality healthcare, and the the members themselves have influence and accountability for healthcare choices.

Politicians (political leaders) benefit because participants and providers have more control over costs and less liability and thus less need for governmental control and legal remedies.

Payors benefit because they spend less time micro-managing patients and providers in order to limit healthcare utilization, and they can spend more time processing claims and reimbursing providers.

Regulators benefit because the healthcare delivery system saves the money usually spent on administration and focuses it on research, review, outcomes, and best practices.

Perhaps the major beneficiaries of community healthcare cooperatives are the 44 million working Americans and their families, including 13 million children, who are currently uninsured. Approximately 36 million Americans work for small organizations that do not provide health coverage because the premiums are prohibitive. Through a community or state healthcare cooperative, everyone's premiums will go down. Participants from small organizations get the same rates as those from big ones. Self-employed people and government-funded participants get the same rate. Thus, everyone will have access to affordable healthcare.

The overall healthcare delivery system should benefit. Instead of the uninsured and underinsured delaying treatment or accessing healthcare through emergency rooms, they can now go to their doctor or community clinic for prevention and early intervention services. This should reduce medical write-offs, cost shifting, and excessive rate increases. Best of all, America's healthcare dollars can be spent on the delivery of healthcare rather than the administration and control of it.

CHAPTER THIRTY-ONE

HOW THE HEALTHCARE TRUST WORKS

A community or state healthcare trust is a 501(C)(9) trust established by Congress as a provision of the Employee Retirement Income Security Act of 1974 (ERISA). As said earlier, the purpose of a VEBA (Voluntary Employer Beneficiary Association) as stated in IRS Section 501(C)(9) is to provide "life, sick, accident and other benefits to safeguard or improve the health of a member or their dependents."

A VEBA is a pre-funded healthcare trust fund. Organizations make periodic tax-deductible contributions to the fund on behalf of their participants. Participants are not taxed when those contributions are made to the fund. Participants can also make contributions to the fund on their own behalf with pretax dollars. Local, state, or federal government can make contributions to the Trust on behalf of its participants.

Only healthcare benefits can be paid from the Trust fund. Trust earnings cannot be paid to anyone. Profit cannot be made or paid to stockholders, executives, employers, or employees. Qualified life, sick, accident, and other benefits can be paid from the fund and are not taxable to the participant. That is, healthcare benefits paid to and for the participant from the

Trust are subject to the same tax treatments as benefits from other healthcare plans.

The Trust can be used to pay retiree benefits and can accumulate reserves to pay for estimated future costs. The Trust fund accumulates interest tax-free further adding to its reserve and usefulness. To qualify for tax-exempt status, the Trust must meet certain requirements:

- Its members must consist of employees or former employees.
- It must be a voluntary association.
- Its members must join voluntarily.
- Its purpose must be to provide life, sick, accident, or other benefits.
- Its benefits must help members and their dependents.
- No part of the earnings can benefit anyone.
- Only qualified healthcare benefits can be paid for or to someone.
- Its benefits must be made available to all members (no class distinction).
- Its benefits must not discriminate in favor of highly compensated employees.
- Its members must have an "employment-related common bond," which means either a
    - √ common employer, or
    - √ affiliated employees, or
    - √ collective bargaining agreement, or
    - √ one or more local labor unions, or
    - √ one or more employees in the same line of business.

An amendment to ERISA would drop the restriction "same line of business" so that **anyone,** including the self-employed and the uninsured, could participate in the community or state collaborative.

The Trust must be controlled by its membership. Members usually designate trustees to direct the Trust on their behalf. Trustees hire staff to manage operations or select external fiduciaries to perform operational functions, such as insurance carriers to insure the participants or third-party administrators to process claims.

❧

CHAPTER THIRTY-TWO

RECIPIENTS OF BENEFITS

Perrmissible recipients of benefits include:

- Members
- Their designated beneficiaries
- Their dependents. IRS regulations define a "dependent" as:
  - The member's spouse
  - Any child of the member who is a minor or student
  - Any child of the spouse who is a minor or student
  - Any child or other minor residing with the member
  - Any other individual considered dependent for federal income tax purposes

CHAPTER THIRTY-THREE

ॐ

PERMISSIBLE BENEFITS

In general, the Trust can provide life, sick, accident, or other benefits in the form of cash or non-cash benefits. To qualify for tax exemption, substantially all of the operations of the Trust must be used to provide permissible healthcare benefits.

A life benefit includes burial benefits and term life insurance. The term policy may contain the right to convert to a whole life policy. A whole life policy is permissible if available to all members and is paid for by the Trust.

Sick and accident benefits are paid for a member or a member's dependent in the event of an illness or injury. Benefits may include disability income during a period when the member cannot work because of sickness or injury. These benefits can be paid directly through reimbursements to a member or a member's dependent, or by paying premiums or fees to an insurance company, medical clinic, or similar program. The Trust can also reimburse retired members for premiums they pay for coverage under Medicare. The amendment to allow **anyone** to participate would allow Medicare- and Medicaid-eligible recipients to participate.

The Trust is designed to safeguard or improve the health of its members and their dependents. Therefore, it can

157

pay for a wide range of wellness benefits, including wellness check-ups and prevention programs, wellness education and fitness activities, health promotion activities and training and childcare. One clarification recommended is that wellness benefits be paid to and provided by a 501(C)(3) charitable, non-profit healthcare organization to ensure access, quality, and reliability.

(The content of the previous sections reflects material written by J. Michael Hines, Esq., and Paul R. Lang, Esq., for the Bureau of National Affairs, Inc. and its Tax Management Tax Practice Services, 1993-1998).

CHAPTER THIRTY-FOUR

PLAN DESIGN

Revenue (Defined Contributions)

Contributions or premiums paid into the Trust may come from organizations, individuals, or governments. For the employed, contributions to the Trust may come from the employer, from the employee, or both. It is a defined contribution plan rather than a defined benefit plan. Organizations make a defined contribution to the Trust on behalf of their participants. The amount is based on an amount per participant. Participants may contribute pretax dollars to the plan either as a fixed amount or percentage of income. The participant contribution makes up the unfunded difference between what the organization contributes and the cost of coverage. Individuals or the self-employed may make tax-deductible contributions (payments) to the fund. Governments (local, state, and national) may make contributions to the fund on behalf of their participants.

Reimbursement: (Four Options)

1. The Trust may offer several plans from several insurance carriers and give participants the option to choose a carrier. The Trust would pay the premium for its participants from the Trust funds.

2. The Trust may contract with a single insurance carrier to provide coverage, process claims, and prepare reports. The Trust would pay the premiums for its participants from the Trust fund.
3. The Trust may contract with providers and then with a third-party administrator to process claims and prepare reports.
4. The Trust may contract directly with providers and then pay providers directly, process claims, prepare aggregate data, and report to trustees and membership.

Coverage: (75/25)

1. Wellness Benefits: The Plan pays 100 percent of usual and customary rates.
2. Center Benefits: The Plan pays 75 to 100 percent of usual and customary rates.
3. Other Benefits: The Plan pays 75 percent of usual and customary rates.
4. Other Benefits: The patient pays 25 percent of usual and customary rates.

Services: (Eight Types)

1. Wellness: Fitness, Education, Activities, Vitamins
2. Clinic: Routine Treatment, Emergency Assessment/Treatment/Referral
3. Hospital: Medical, Surgical
4. Professional: Physician, Therapist, Nurses, Hospice
5. Diagnostic: Laboratory, X-Rays, MRI, CT Scans, EKGs
6. Ancillary: Home Health, Equipment, Supplies
7. Pharmaceutical: Local, Mail Order
8. Dental: Preventive, Treatment, Orthodontics

CHAPTER THIRTY-FIVE

COMMUNITY HEALTH CENTERS

Community health centers will be located in communities throughout the country. These centers can be free-standing or located in or adjacent to churches, synagogues, mosques, schools, drug stores, recreation centers, day-care centers, or post offices. Ideally, community health centers should be located in an existing faith-based or community organization to reduce the cost of overhead and operations.

The community health center could also be located in or near a local senior citizen's center or recreation that already has utilities and support staff to minimize any additional costs of operation.

Community health centers could be added to faith-based organizations, especially those that have day-care centers, food banks, clothes closets, or activity centers. These facilities already have available parking, are known in the community, and usually have ample classroom, kitchen, and meeting space available during the week. People in the neighborhood or community are accustomed to attending these facilities and they are well established with an existing high level of trust and confidence. These organizations provide several points of contact in the community to help facilitate establishing community health centers.

The community health center provides a place for people in the community to have affordable access to healthcare. People could come to the center for free wellness programs. The community health center provides wellness programs focused on nutrition, exercise, health assessments, health education, and life management, as well as financial and legal planning, prenatal classes, and care-giving classes. All would be a part of the wellness programs offered through community health centers.

The community health center would also provide basic medical services to include diagnostic and medical treatment services, routine medical exams, minor surgery, treatment of surface wounds, medical management, and medical information. They would also treat and refer appropriate medical, surgical, and emergency services to area hospitals. Low-income participants could access basic healthcare and pharmaceutical services at little or no cost to them or to their families.

Providers would include physicians, physician assistants, nurse practitioners, nurses, nursing assistants, licensed professional clinicians, psychologists, licensed professional social workers, nutritionists, and pharmacists.

The center would reimburse providers at 100 percent of usual and customary charges. Providers could offer services on a pro bono basis. Retired healthcare professionals could provide assistance for the center, especially retired nurses, physicians, therapists, pharmacists, etc. Local faith-based organizations could give additional support specifically for their members participating or seeking treatment as well as make in-kind or direct contributions to support the center.

In essence, the community health center becomes not only the first line of defense in treating illnesses, but more important, the first line of offense in promoting wellness. The community health center enables the American healthcare system to deliver healthcare directly to where people live in their community. It takes healthcare out to the urban or suburban neighborhood, small town, rural community, mountain hamlet, or Indian Reservation. It makes quality healthcare accessible to everyone, regardless of where they live. It makes quality healthcare affordable regardless of how little money they make. It makes quality, accessible, affordable healthcare a reality in every community. It makes quality, accessible, affordable healthcare a responsibility for every community.

Participants would be expected to pay directly either by cash, check, credit card or from their healthcare savings account using a Medical debit card. Participants would be expected to pay from 1 percent to 25 percent of usual and customary charges based on the their ability to pay.

Participants would have open and unlimited access to the center. They would be expected to fill out basic paperwork.

Local, state, and federal government would continue to provide ongoing support as well. Additional support could come from philanthropic sources, local and regional organizations, and hospitals, businesses, even pharmaceutical companies and faith-based institutions. Services would be based on participants' ability to pay. The community health center could sell supplies, using a portion of the proceeds from the sales to supplement the cost of operations.

In addition, the sale of other items produced at or for the centers, such as crafts, furniture, art, blankets, quilts, baked goods, etc., could also be used to reduce overhead costs and operations of the center itself. Community health centers could provide gift shops and health stores with proceeds to benefit the center and feature local arts and crafts on consignment.

Participants who have a limited amount of income might be encouraged or even required to provide community service or assistance to the center, perhaps working as secretary, receptionist, security guard, general volunteer, giving janitorial maintenance assistance, helping with or making arts and crafts, etc., to help provide additional income for the center's overall viability and to fulfill their financial responsibility.

CHAPTER THIRTY-SIX

H E L P Teams

Health Assessment
Wellness Education
Life Management
Financial Planning

A. Mission

Take it to the people! Take (HELP) health assessments, wellness education, life management, and financial planning directly to the people who need it. Partner with community organizations to provide HELP to people where they live and work, play and pray.

We are in the third year of a major transition in healthcare. It is the single biggest shift in sixty years. We are rapidly moving from a plan-driven/payor controlled healthcare system to a consumer-driven/patient-controlled healthcare delivery system. Consumer-directed or patient-directed healthcare means the patient and his family along with their physician will determine what and how much illness treatment people will utilize. Defined Contribution Health Plans are, according to *Employee Benefit News*, moving swiftly and forcefully across the benefits industry.

What this means is that health assessments, wellness education, life management and financial planning are now more important than ever. Yet people have less time than ever to obtain this invaluable information. Hence, to help them and help all of us, we need to take this HELP to the people.

For the last fifteen years we have been taking these opportunities to the workplace through health fairs, lunch and learns, and work/life seminars. While we have offered these off-site and after hours, fewer and fewer people have been able to come because of busy schedules. Instead, we have taken them to the workplace. Now, we want to take a two-hour, high-intensity version of these programs to the other places people meet: churches, synagogues, clubs, and community organizations.

B. Strategy

The strategy is reminiscent of the way education, healthcare, and community services were delivered years ago. Small communities provided education and healthcare directly to people through faith-based and community organizations. For a time, churches, schools, and the neighborhood store were the center of the community.

This strategy also underscores what is called a life matrix, i.e., the connections between faith, finances, health, wellness, work and life.

- Our faith affects our finances, health, wellness, work, and life.
- Our finances affect our faith, health, wellness, work, and life.
- Our health affects our faith, finances, wellness, work, and life.
- Our wellness affects our work, life, health, faith, and finances.
- Our life obviously affects our finances, work, health, wellness, and faith.

	FAITH	FINANCES	HEALTH	WELLNESS	WORK	LIFE
FAITH						
FINANCES						
HEALTH						
WELLNESS						
WORK						
LIFE						

This initiative will encourage and facilitate health assessments, wellness education, life management, and financial planning seminars to occur where people live and work, play and pray. We've learned from the workplace that people will attend a workshop if it's provided at the work site during company time. The same can be said of churches and other "faith places." People will attend a workshop if it's convenient. They will get HELP, that is, they will get **H**ealth assessment, health **E**ducation, **L**ife management training, and legal and financial **P**lanning if it's done where they and their families already gather.

HELP teams would provide two hours of life education, primarily in "faith places," once a year over a five-year period. A team of four professionals would provide people with an opportunity to attend four half-hour seminars which would include:

1. Health assessments for an annual benchmarking
2. Health education on five levels
3. Life management training in five key areas
4. Financial and legal planning in five basic areas

1. Health Assessments

These are basic, external health assessments—blood pressure screening, weight analysis, healthcare questionnaire, and stress test. The score on these four instruments would serve as benchmarks for people to measure their progress each year in each of these areas.

2. Health Education

- Child Health (prenatal care, immunizations, nutrition)
- Teen Stuff (body talk, sex education, food and nutrition, risk management)
- Adult Talk (prevention, healthcare, medications, nutrition)
- Midlife Matters (menopause, heart conditions, medications)
- Senior Issues (diagnosis, treatment, protocols, disease management)

3. Life Management

- Money management
- Stress management
- Conflict management
- Time management
- Family management

4. Financial Planning

- Money Strategies (how to make, save, spend, and invest money wisely)
- Insurance Strategies (life, health, disability, automobile, home, property, and long-term care)
- Property Strategies (home ownership, rental property, land, real estate trusts, burial plots)
- Investment Strategies (money market accounts, certificate of deposits, insurance, stocks, bonds, futures, mutual funds)
- Estate Planning (wills, trusts, property arrangements, death arrangements, funeral arrangements, living wills, medical durable power of attorney)

C. Methodology

With over 700 faith-based organizations in our community, the opportunity to take this initial program and move it throughout the community is most significant.

D. Request

Once a year, faith-based and not-for-profit organizations in the community may provide two hours of HELP during a regular time in which they meet: Sunday 10:00 a.m.-12:00 noon, Wednesday 6:30 p.m.-8:30 p.m., Saturday 10:00 a.m.-12:00 noon, a lunch-and-learn meeting Monday through Saturday, a breakfast meeting one Saturday morning or one day during the week.

Participants could attend each of the four half-hour microshops:

1. **H**ealth Assessment,
2. Health **E**ducation,
3. **L**ife Management,
4. Financial **P**lanning

The cost to financially support each team is $500: $100 per presenter ($400) plus $100 administrative support (supplies, materials, postage, travel, and other related expenses). The goal is to present forty seminars in a year.

Asbury United Methodist Church, located in a transitional neighborhood in Oakland Park, provides a good example of how effectively this strategy has worked and how it can be implemented throughout the city of Columbus and across the country. Life and health seminars have been presented on Sunday morning during Sunday school and morning worship services, as well as on youth retreats. These workshops have helped at-risk young people deal with the challenges of living in at-risk neighborhoods and being in an at-risk population. These seminars have helped older adults deal with aging in America, especially if they are widows of military personnel who came from other countries and now have difficulty with the language and economy of this country.

We wish to take the successful model used at Asbury and expand it throughout the area. This model could have application and implications far beyond this region.

Chapter Thirty-Seven

How Is the Cooperative Funded?

In general, community or state healthcare cooperatives will utilize existing guidelines, regulations, and auditing procedures as prescribed by current ERISA regulations. The Trust must be established at a federally insured (FDIC) financial institution. The funds deposited in it belong solely to the Trust for the participants and cannot be used for any other purpose except healthcare benefits for its participants. The amount in reserve is specifically regulated. Healthcare trusts have been extensively used across the country by large and medium-sized organizations since 1974.

Unlike Multiple Employer Welfare Associations (MEWA) or Association Health Plans (AHP), community or state healthcare cooperatives will be established under already existing federal guidelines, rules, regulations, reserves, and auditing procedures. ERISA law and IRS rulings dictate the practice and procedures of these trusts. Moreover, their operations and oversight fall under the purview of at least four major federal agencies—the Internal Revenue Service, the Department of Justice, the Department of Labor, and the Department of Health and Human Services as well as state insurance commissions and licensing agencies.

If Congress will amend the current ERISA law to allow anyone to join a Community or State Healthcare Cooperative, then everyone in a community or state could potentially participate. A defined contribution may be made by the participants or the organization of the participant or by some other entity or individual or by the government.

ERISA currently states that 90 percent of the participants must be employed or retired. Employees can be from large companies, small companies, not-for-profit organizations, government entities, professional groups, professional practices or be self-employed. It is proposed that Congress authorize one to five alpha states to initiate the Cooperatives.

State Healthcare Cooperatives could then be offered in all 50 states and include both Medicaid- and Medicare-eligible participants. The government would pay the defined contributions for Medicaid and Medicare participants.

Defined contributions for the unemployed would be made from each state's unemployment insurance fund. Medicare, Medicaid, and unemployed patients would be responsible for up to 25 percent of the charges, which may be paid from their Healthcare Savings Account (HSA) and/or supplemented by the patient, relatives, providers, local government, charities or a Healthcare Benevolent Fund. People may also utilize community health centers where appropriate medical services are provided based on the participants' ability to pay. Providers may also choose to write off patient balances as charity care.

Contributions to the Community or State Healthcare Cooperative are tax deductible. The trustees of the Trust set the amount per participant. The Trust is established at a commercial bank or an appropriate federally insured financial institution.

Trustees for the fund must be participants in the Healthcare Cooperative, be employed persons, and be participants in the Trust itself. They are trustees of the fund and represent all other participants. They have a fiduciary and oversight responsibility for the Trust but cannot be paid for their services. They may hire others to manage the day-to-day operations of the Cooperative. One trustee is elected for every 10,000 participants in the Cooperative. Organizations with over 10,000 employees can nominate qualified and specially trained participants to serve in trustee positions. However, they must be elected by the entire membership.

The Trust itself is guaranteed with cash or cash equivalents and/or unencumbered fixed assets, such as building and property. The initial requirement recommended is $1 million in cash or $10 million of unencumbered fixed capital. The fixed capital should originate from multiple stakeholders, such as hospitals, business, or government. The Trust is further guaranteed with $10 in cash or cash equivalents per participant, or $100 of unencumbered fixed capital per participant.

Reinsurance for the Trust is mandatory and can be purchased from the funds committed. Major stop loss coverage is a requirement.

CHAPTER THIRTY-EIGHT

FUNDING OPTION A: PREMIUM PAID BY MULTIPLE SOURCES

Organizations (employers, governments) may contribute all or a portion of the required amount on behalf of their participants. Participants must contribute the difference. The self-employed would contribute the entire portion. All contributions are tax deductible whether from the employer or the employee. Participants could be employed by big companies, by small businesses, be self-employed, be employed in not-for-profit or government organizations, or be Medicare or Medicaid recipients.

Assume the cost of healthcare is $3,000 per participant per year. Organizations would be required to contribute $3,000 per participant. The self-employed person would be required to contribute $3,000.

Can organizations or participants contribute more than the required amount? The answer is yes. The extra contribution from the organization can accumulate in a general reserve or a restricted reserve for the specific organization to use during difficult economic times. Participants can contribute extra to their own Healthcare Savings Account (HSA). Contributions and interest are tax deductible. However, funds can only be used for healthcare purposes.

CHAPTER THIRTY-NINE

FUNDING OPTION B: PREMIUM PAID BY THE GOVERNMENT

An alternate method of funding would be government funding of the annual premium for each covered life. The government contributes the annual premium for each covered life within the community or state. Seventy-five percent of the contribution goes into the general fund, while 25 percent goes into an individual's (covered life) Healthcare Savings Account. Individuals and/or organizations can contribute additional amounts to an individual's or employee's H.S.A. Such contributions would still be tax deductible to the contributor and a non-taxable event to the participant.

With this funding option, the government makes the defined contribution to cover the premium for each person (resident/covered life). The premium is for each person (man, woman, or child) within the community or state. Currently the average premium for <u>each person</u> would be $3,000.

Local, state, and federal entities already pay the premiums for local, state, and federal employees and their dependents; D.O.D. and V.A.-eligible people and their dependents; Medicare- and Medicaid-eligible people and their dependents; and incarcerated and indigent people and their dependents. That leaves the privately insured population, for which the government would need to collect additional revenue to pay their premiums.

One method to cover these expenses is with a state sales tax. Thus, every person in America—whether living, working, studying, or visiting this country—would be involved in funding a healthcare system that can be accessed by anyone and everyone. Every person who has access to and/or uses the system ought to make a contribution to it or have a financial stake in the utilization of it.

CHAPTER FORTY

HOW DOES THE COOPERATIVE FUNCTION?

Seventy-five percent of the total contributed amount ($2,250) is used to fund the general healthcare coverage of all participants annually. Twenty-five percent of the amount contributed ($750) is placed in a participant's Healthcare Savings Account. Participants may use their HSA each year to pay the co-payment for healthcare services they receive. The unused amount in the HSA is rolled over to the next year. Additional contributions are made to the HSA each year by the individual, organization, or government.

Seventy-five percent of the defined contribution is deposited in the general fund of the Trust. From that fund, 100 percent of all wellness and clinic services and 75 percent of all other healthcare services, procedures, and products are paid.

Twenty-five percent of the defined contribution is deposited in the participant's Healthcare Savings Account. The account is held in the Trust for the sole benefit of the participants. As such, the HSA "belongs" to the participant. It accrues with interest tax-free. If an organization contributes the full or partial amount, it is tax deductible to the organization and tax-free to the participant. However, it can only be used for healthcare services, procedures and products.

No exceptions! Unused portions of this HSA roll over to the next year.

Catastrophic coverage would be purchased by or through an insurance carrier or provided directly by the Cooperative.

A separate benevolent fund will be established to assist with catastrophic medical cases. It could be funded by participant's donations, corporate and philanthropic donations, and/or by an acceptable formulary (such as 1 percent of the 75 percent contributed to the general fund). Participants with major medical expenses may request from the benevolent fund, all or part of the 25 percent for which they are financially responsible. Disbursement guidelines would be established to guide the benevolent fund committee that could include criteria such as medical necessity, age, efficacy, lifestyle, and financial need.

Chapter Forty-One

Stakeholder Interest

Stakeholder #1: Purchasers

Why would large, multi-state organizations be interested in Community or State Healthcare Cooperatives? Large organizations are interested because of cost, quality, and uniformity. Increasing participation increases the economics of scale and population (risk) pool, giving greater purchasing leverage. Large organizations with good benefits are already being forced to supplement participants from small organizations or the self-employed when spouses choose to go to work for or remain with them. People who already have or anticipate large medical expenses migrate to or remain with organizations for good healthcare benefits. Designing a system where everyone can participate actually saves large organizations money.

Large organizations also realize that this nation cannot leave one of every seven Americans (44 million people) uninsured, and another two out of seven (80 million people) underinsured. If major organizations fail to help solve the healthcare problem, then the federal government will, which will lead to exploding expenses financed by increased taxes, with no reward for wellness and healthy lifestyles.

Large organizations across multiple states would welcome similar plans in each state. Moreover, large organizations would appreciate plans where participants take more control, responsibility, and accountability for their own health. Large organizations could also anticipate their healthcare costs more accurately. Their healthcare expenses are limited to their defined contribution per participant. Another plus for large self-funded organizations is that they are no longer liable for the fund, nor must they pay for the administration of it or pay for IRS audits of it. A big plus is such a plan will reduce and may eliminate the costs, hassles, and liability for companies to be HIPAA compliant.

Unions should be pleased with Community Healthcare Cooperatives. They actually helped create them. VEBAs were originally designed with organized labor (unions) in mind. People had to have "an employment-related common bond" or "collective bargaining agreement" or "be in one or more local labor unions." The two biggest issues for union members today are job security and cost of healthcare. Plus, the latter affects the former. Making and keeping healthcare available and affordable for its members is a huge issue for unions. Moreover, the employer's contribution remains a matter of contract negotiation. It is still a "term and condition" of the bargaining agreement.

It's obvious why small business would be very interested in a Community or State Healthcare Cooperative. It would enable them to obtain good healthcare coverage for their employees at the same rate and quality available to major corporations. Smaller employers could accurately budget their annual healthcare expense per year per employee—based on a defined contribution per employee. Smaller employers would benefit from the leverage, expertise, and advocacy available only to large employers. Their healthcare costs are stabilized year after year. They are not the victim of experienced-based rates, but participate instead in community or state-based rates.

By paying at least some of the cost of their employee healthcare premiums, small organizations could actually help solve the problem of the uninsured instead of contributing to it. By providing healthcare coverage, they could actually attract and keep good people, especially those who need and must have health coverage.

The self-employed would be very pleased to belong to a Community or State Healthcare Cooperative. They can actually obtain affordable, quality healthcare coverage for themselves and their families. The rates and benefits would be equal to that which is currently only available to larger organizations.

Stakeholder #2: Providers

Providers would definitely welcome Community or State Healthcare Cooperatives. They want a simplified, reasonable, timely, affordable healthcare system. Providers want adequate coverage for all their patients. Providers will serve as or consult with trustees of the Cooperative to design, implement, and manage the Cooperative. Providers would also welcome a plan that rewards healthy lifestyles. Providers want affordable, quality healthcare coverage for themselves, their families and their employees.

Stakeholder #3: Participants

Why would people want to participate in such a plan? First, the Cooperative provides medical coverage at reasonable rates. It pays for wellness expenses, activities, and products. It rewards people for healthy lifestyles. It encourages people to be better consumers of healthcare. It enables them to save money (in Healthcare Savings Accounts) for things such as the birth of a child, major surgery, illness, or medical services during retirement.

Young, single people will like the Cooperative because the participant-only coverage is relatively inexpensive and may be fully paid for by the contribution from the employer. Then

25 percent of that contribution goes into the participant's HSA. Wellness activities and products are paid for by the plan at 100 percent, so the balance with interest rolls to the next year. It grows exponentially until they need it. Yet nearly 75 percent of the employer's contribution is going into a general pool to provide for other people in the community. All of them, or their employers, are contributing the same amount and that fund is portable.

Participants with dependents like it because it provides affordable, quality healthcare. Their employer may make the full contribution for the employee while the employee through payroll deduction pays the remainder for family coverage. Wellness and health center services for the whole family are paid up to 100 percent by the plan. Twenty-five percent of the total contribution goes into an HSA. The unused portion plus interest is rolled over to the next year. That money is portable, tax-free, and can be used only for healthcare.

Stakeholder #4: Relatives

Relatives should welcome a Community or State Healthcare Cooperative because it offers reasonable, affordable, quality healthcare coverage for their family. Relatives may be uncomfortable, however, with the new responsibility inherent in Community or State Healthcare Cooperatives. No longer will a relative or patient be able to say to the doctor "do everything possible" and expect someone else to pay for it. Now, all medical decisions by patients and relatives will have a personal family financial element to them. There will be times when enough is enough.

Stakeholder #5: Payors

Payors provide healthcare information, verify eligibility, process claims, track utilization, prepare reports, and monitor providers. Participants choose a healthcare provider and healthcare service. They discuss with the provider the anticipated fees. The provider submits the claims. The plan pays 75 percent of usual and customary charges; the participant pays the 25 percent co-payment from their HSA by check, credit card, or in monthly payments. The provider provides the service and submits a claim. The payor processes the claim.

Much of the process can be done electronically or with a medical debit card. Providers, physicians, nurses, and staff no longer need to spend endless hours negotiating services for their patients. Payors no longer need large staffs, especially professional staffs, to manage care, control access, limit services, deny claims, battle providers, and face lawsuits. Payors and providers may be able to release professional staff to practice medicine rather than micro-manage treatment. If the micro-managing of care has doubled the administrative expenses of healthcare (increased the staff, office space, equipment, supplies of physician practices, hospital services, ancillary programs, insurance carriers, and third-party administrators), then the user-friendly system of Community or State Healthcare Cooperatives could save over $200 billion in wasted healthcare expenses each year.

Over $400 billion of the $1.6 trillion spent on healthcare each year is spent on the administration of illness care. By putting the participant back in charge and by dramatically simplifying the reimbursement process, we could free $300 to $500 billion each year to better pay good providers, offer more services to participants, minimize cost increases to purchasers, and even give payors ways to make a profit.

Payors are not only welcoming the shift to defined contribution healthcare plans, they are pursuing such plans. Aetna, Humana, Blue Cross/Blue Shield, Wellpoint, Definity, and Lumenos have developed and are marketing defined contribution healthcare plans. A Community or State Healthcare Cooperative takes them three steps forward.

Stakeholders #6: Politicians

A big plus for political leaders is they do not have to raise taxes or engage in political warfare to provide for community or statewide healthcare. Community or State Healthcare Cooperatives could offer affordable, quality healthcare to government employees and serve as a vehicle for serving the uninsured and the Medicare and Medicaid populations. Most of all, VEBAs already exist. Political leaders do not have to reinvent the wheel. Community or State Healthcare Cooperatives avoid the need for a patient's bill of rights. Political leaders are very interested in Community or State Healthcare Cooperatives because they see the opportunity to provide healthcare to the entire nation especially to most of the 44 million uninsured of which 80 percent are working. By supporting Community or State Healthcare Cooperatives, political leaders may actually reduce the misuse of the healthcare system…uninsured people going to the emergency room for routine medical treatment or people committing crimes to access healthcare through the judicial system.

Stakeholder #7: Regulators

Regulators will, over all, appreciate Community or State Healthcare Cooperatives. Because these are VEBA Trusts, they fall under federal guidelines and federal jurisdiction. The rules, the regulations, and the enforcement mechanisms already exist. It means that healthcare plans would be consistent across the country. Health plans (Trusts) would be governed by the U.S. Department of Labor and the Department of Health and Human Services, audited by the Internal Revenue Service, and held accountable by the U.S. Department of Justice as well as state insurance commissions and regulatory agencies.

Participants, providers, purchaser, payors, and politicians are all winners because Community or State Healthcare Cooperatives reduce the costs and hassles of providing healthcare, illness treatment, and wellness services. The high cost of micro-managing or overcontrolling healthcare is dramatically reduced in this plan.

However, the biggest winners are the participants. They help design the plan directly or through their elected, designated, or appointed Trustees. The plan design is remarkably easy to understand. It covers 100 percent of the cost for wellness programs, services, and products, as well as services at community health centers, plus 75 percent of all other healthcare and illness treatment products, services, and procedures. The plan rewards healthy lifestyles. Moreover, the unused portion of the participant's Healthcare Savings Account accrues tax-free interest and rolls over to the next year. The Healthcare Savings Account belongs to the participant, it is portable, and it can be used for further healthcare needs and expenses.

❧

Chapter Forty-Two

Management Mechanism

A State Healthcare Cooperative falls under existing ERISA guidelines. As such, it becomes a stand-alone Trust at a federally insured financial institution. All deposits are guaranteed. Trustees are elected to serve as a representative Trustee of the Plan. Only employed or retired persons can be Trustees of the Trust and must be participants as well. They may serve five-year terms and a maximum of two consecutive terms. Trustees, in turn, hire others to manage the plan.

Such a structure complies with current ERISA and VEBA laws and regulations. The Internal Revenue Service, U.S. Department of Labor, the Department of Health and Human Services, and the U.S. Department of Justice provide oversight. Yet, the State Healthcare Cooperative still provides for local control, responsibility, and accountability. Participants serve as Trustees and have a compelling interest in the viability and continuity of the Cooperative. Members include participants, providers, purchasers, payors, politicians, regulators, and relatives. All stakeholders are in the Healthcare Cooperative and have a stake in its service and success.

A State Healthcare Cooperative is similar to a community or state credit union. All participants are members. These participants make a deposit into the credit union, usually electronically. Funds may be split (e.g., into a savings account and/or to pay off a loan). Board members are elected and they govern the credit union, set policy and procedures, hire staff, and hold them accountable. Periodic reports are required. Oversight and reporting comes from the IRS, the Federal Credit Union, and various federal and state regulatory agencies.

Statewide Healthcare Cooperatives would hold all funds in a Trust. Trustees must be employed or retired persons (not of the Trust) voluntarily participating in the cooperative. Trustees are elected to represent 10,000 other participants. Large organizations and unions may nominate representatives based on the number of people for whom they are making defined contributions (at least 100 percent of participant-only coverage). Participants from small organizations and the self-employed would nominate one representative per 10,000 participants.

The Trustees would submit the list of nominees to the entire membership for annual election, including officers and an executive committee. Trustees would hire management and staff depending on the model used for paying claims—single insurer, multiple insurers, third-party administrator, or internal claims administrator.

The Trustees would also have ultimate responsibility for plan design and claims administration. The general framework for all plans is as follows:

1. Wellness benefits covered by the plan at 100 percent; participant pays 0.
2. Center benefits covered by the plan up to 100 percent; participant pays 0 to 25 percent.
3. Hospital benefits covered by the plan at 75 percent; participant pays 25 percent.
4. Professional benefits covered by the plan at 75 percent; participant pays 25 percent.

5. Dental benefits covered by the plan at 75 percent; participant pays 25 percent.
6. Ancillary benefits covered by the plan at 75 percent; participant pays 25 percent.
7. Pharmaceutical benefits covered by the plan at 75 percent; participant pays 25 percent.
8. Diagnostic benefits covered by the plan at 75 percent; participant pays 25 percent.

The Plan operates with no deductible and high out-of-pocket limits. Trustees along with providers, payors, and their management team negotiate reimbursement rates. The rates should reimburse all providers fairly and be based on regional or national norms (e.g., RBRVS, Milliman, etc.). These rates, along with provider rating, are made available to all participants in the Cooperative. The recommended providers pledge not to charge participants beyond the agreed-upon rate unless the higher rate is negotiated between the participant and the provider.

The Trustees, along with participants, providers, payors, regulators, the management team, and the appropriate local, state, and national association establish a Recommended Provider Network. No provider is excluded unless there are serious, verifiable charges or association actions against him or her. Increasingly, peers, patients, payors, and purchasers will rate providers for quality, service, and value. The Recommended Provider Network will be available online with provider pictures and service profiles, hours, location, charges, ratings, and recommendations plus a Web link, address, and telephone number.

Trustees are also the Plan fiduciaries. They must make and maintain the Trust's financial viability. They set the annual cost per participant for member-only, member plus one, and member plus family. These rates must be fair, just, equitable, and defensible. These rates cannot discriminate because of age, race, religion, gender, family status, economic status, or position. The rates cannot favor the highly compensated.

The Trustees, after extensive negotiation and ample notification, will have the authority to raise overall participant premiums. Participants and all other stakeholders will have ample opportunity to participate in discussion, review the factors, provide recommendations, and review the causes for a premium increase. Trust participants will be asked to vote on healthcare exclusions, restrictions, incentives, and/or sanctions.

CHAPTER FORTY-THREE

PROFESSIONAL COOPERATION

Essential to providing quality, affordable healthcare to everyone is professional cooperation. Indeed, professionals from all disciplines must cooperate to successfully improve access to quality, affordable, effective healthcare. This cooperation includes professionals from medicine, law, accounting, business, theology, and science. Most important is the cooperation between health professionals and legal professionals.

Closely connected to the political and regulatory stakeholders is the legal profession. In fact, they become participants in healthcare by advising, representing, or suing purchasers, providers, or payors. The high cost of legal services, excessive awards, and liability insurance is a major factor in driving up the cost of healthcare and driving providers, payors, and purchasers out of business.

Lawyers are also personal participants in healthcare. They must or should provide coverage and benefits for themselves, their staffs, and their families. More significant, they or a member of their family may become a patient in the illness treatment system. They want and need the system to be affordable, reliable, usable, and effective.

Even attorneys agree that we must address the litigious and contentious environment in which medicine operates. We must realign legal strategies with health strategies. We must encourage health and wellness, access and affordability, responsibility and accountability, protection and correction.

Legal strategies and health strategies must encourage providers to enter the healthcare profession, promote health, encourage wellness, practice good medicine, be patient-sensitive, involve relatives and clergy, and encourage patient responsibility and accountability. Health professionals must themselves practice good medicine and discipline colleagues who do not. Legal strategies and health strategies must encourage patients to take far more responsibility and accountability for their health decisions, lifestyle choices, wellness priorities, and financial exposure.

Legal strategies and health strategies must encourage payors to process claims promptly, verify eligibility, protect patient's privacy, respect provider's credibility, report outcomes impartially, and hold abusers accountable. Health professionals and legal professionals must be guardians of the law, protectors of the innocent, punishers of the guilty, and defenders of the conscientious. Legal providers and health providers must work together to protect and retain good, conscientious, caring providers and payors.

The following proposal combines the best legal strategies with the best health strategies. It is proposed that only the one who is truly injured or harmed by another be permitted to bring a lawsuit to recover economic damages. Economic damages would include all past, present, and future medical and ancillary expenses including hospital, physician, diagnostic, rehabilitation, pharmaceutical, dental, therapeutic, legal, accounting, equipment, supplies, extra care, and healthcare-related expenditures. All expenses related to the injury, including compensation for lost income, would be considered economic damages. Economic damages would also include all anticipated future expenses directly related to the injury and the recovery process. Once all pending bills are paid, the balance of the settlement is placed in the participant's Healthcare Savings Account and grows with interest, tax-free. However, funds from the HSA can only be used to pay healthcare-related expenses.

Compensatory damage payments for "pain and suffering" become obsolete. All medication and treatment for medical pain plus future needs for medical treatment is anticipated, projected, and included in the financial settlement or award. All clinically defined emotional suffering and the subsequent need for clinical treatment is anticipated, projected, and included in the financial settlement.

However, punitive damages and the need to bring suit for such damages remain in effect. A provider or payor can be sued for punitive damages. Punitive damages are awarded for willful neglect or criminal intent. If found guilty, providers or payors could be imprisoned or fined up to 100 percent of their previous year's annual revenue. Hence, the dollar amount of the lawsuit is proportional to the size and revenue of the provider or payor.

Following the guidelines of the Constitution, only the government has the right and responsibility to punish its inhabitants who harm other citizens. Those people who are found guilty of harming other citizens are either imprisoned or fined for the their action. Depending on the "crime" and jurisdiction, the fines are paid to the respective governmental entity.

Punitive damages are financial awards intended to punish. They are fines imposed on guilty people who have harmed or committed a crime against someone. If some person or organization has by willful neglect or criminal intent brought harm to an innocent person, those people responsible deserve to be punished. They should be put in a local, state, or federal prison and/or pay their fine to a local, state or federal fund.

Neither the lawyer(s) nor plaintiff(s) should receive fines—"punishment money." Plaintiffs should be fully compensated for all valid current and future economic damages. Attorneys should be paid fully for all actual and billable expenses. Both parties should pay court costs. The client whom the attorney is representing should pay legal fees. In fact, it could be argued that such cases could be brought by local, state or federal prosecutors.

Valid lawsuits ought to be brought against providers and payors for egregious acts, whether from willful neglect or criminal intent. Good attorneys who represent valid plaintiffs need to be paid for their time and expenses. Patients need to be made economically whole both now and in the future. However, neither patients nor lawyers should get rich over the understandable and legitimate mistakes of others nor should attorneys or patients abuse the whole healthcare system for their own personal financial enrichment.

Legal professionals and health professionals must work together to facilitate an affordable, reliable, user-friendly healthcare system. We will all be better for it and from it.

CHAPTER FORTY-FOUR

IMPLEMENTATION

Legislation to enable State Healthcare Cooperatives is recommended to Congress. For the Cooperative to work, Congress must pass the enabling legislation. Legislation is passed to amend ERISA to allow "anyone in the same geographical area" to participate in a Cooperative. Moreover, Congress passes legislation to support participant-owned Healthcare Savings Accounts (HSA) in the Trust with rollover and portability provisions.

Target at least one, no more than five, alpha states nationwide to implement State Healthcare Cooperatives. The recommended states are Georgia, Arizona, Pennsylvania, Indiana, and Washington. Then expand State Healthcare Cooperatives to all fifty states.

CHAPTER FORTY-FIVE

HEALTHCARE NETWORK, INC.

Healthcare Network, Inc. is a network of people committed to health. While not at all necessary to the creation and implementation of Community or State Healthcare Cooperatives, such a network could benefit participants, relatives, providers, purchasers, payors, politicians, and regulators.

Healthcare Network, Inc, is a not-for-profit association of people who are committed to health.

All the stakeholders of healthcare are permitted and encouraged to participate. Thus purchasers, providers, payors, politicians, regulators, participants, and relatives may participate. These stakeholders access healthcare information as well as influence plan design, product development, service improvement, health promotion, and public policy. The network represents nor advocates for any single group of stakeholders.

Three levels of membership exist: general, professional, and organizational.

General members are individuals who want access to medically approved information on healthcare issues. General members may also help improve the healthcare delivery system in which they are involved as well as influence local, state, and national healthcare policy and legislation.

Professional members are healthcare professionals who are credentialed and licensed and want to be listed in a local, state, and national registry of recommended healthcare providers. Professional members may also access and participate in all the services available to general members. Professional members will also have an active voice in shaping healthcare policy and legislation and improving healthcare services and reimbursement.

Organizational members may provide to their employees and their families all the healthcare information and services available to general members. Plus organizational executives will be invited to participate in local, state, regional, and national healthcare summits to exchange ideas, make recommendations, and shape public policies.

Healthcare Network, Inc. will serve as a clearing site for healthcare information, stakeholder surveys, and medical reports. It will provide a link to other sites and sources of quality, reliable healthcare information and wellness programs. It will provide a national registry of recommended healthcare providers based on credentials, licensure, location, specialty, and clinical record. In the future the registry will include ratings, charges, and outcomes.

Healthcare Network, Inc. will serve as a resource to Community or State Healthcare Cooperatives providing assistance in planning, designing, organizing, initiating, implementing, managing, and evaluating their respective Cooperatives. It will monitor the service of Cooperatives and make recommendations or orchestrate changes accordingly. Healthcare Network, Inc. will also encourage support of local chapters and state associations. These local chapters and state organizations will facilitate local and state healthcare summits to enhance the relationships among stakeholders as well as encourage mutually beneficial public policies, reimbursement procedures, and healthcare strategies.

PART FOUR

THE REVOLUTION HAS BEGUN

FIRST CALL

In October of 1994, the Columbus Chapter of the American Association of Management Accountants were introduced to the fifteen forces or factors that would change the way healthcare would be delivered in this country.

A Revolution was coming!

LEADERSHIP COLUMBUS

In May of 1999, Leadership Columbus participants were told that a "comet" was coming that would change the way healthcare is delivered in this country. The image used was based on the movie *Deep Impact*. They were told that the healthcare comet would be patient-controlled healthcare.

Twelve forces were identified that would create major changes in the way healthcare would be delivered. The first force was medical costs. In 1999, they were already anticipating an increase of 6 to 10 percent. The second force was patients and relatives who had experiences with managed care that ranged from bad to horrible to criminal because of poor service, long waits, lengthy paperwork, and endless forms. Hence, a growing number of Americans were in an uproar over managed care, which leads to the third force: state and federal legislation.

In 1998, ten members of Congress were elected on a platform of healthcare reform. By 1999, over a dozen bills were introduced in both houses of Congress broadly categorized as the Patient's Bill of Rights. In the summer of 1999, one bill passed in the House and another bill passed in the Senate—HR2990, called the Norwood-Dingle Bill, and S1344, called the Patient's Bill of Rights. It was not a question of whether there would there be a Patient's Bill of Rights; it was a question of who would be sued and for how much.

The fourth factor changing the way healthcare would be delivered in this country was Dickie Scruggs and his army of law firms. Having successfully defeated the tobacco industiry, he was prepared to take on managed care plans across the country. The fifth factor was medical technology and the ability to do almost an infinite amount of things to a human body to keep it alive, but at what cost and paid by whom? The sixth factor was medical knowledge. Access to the Internet was making available to patients and relatives more medical information regarding diagnosis, procedures, and protocols than ever before, which leads to the seventh factor: consumerism. With that access to information, patients would demand more control over the decisions about their healthcare.

Leadership Columbus participants were given the eighth factor—medical disparity. There are not only financial disparities—meaning some people with money can have access to healthcare and others without money do not. But there is a geographical disparity—rural areas and urban centers are being left out of the increased medical services provided to people in suburbs. The ninth factor presented was the aging population, especially the growing number of people over the age of eighty and the massive numbers of Baby Boomers who will overwhelm our healthcare delivery system in the next twenty to fifty years. The tenth factor, on the other end of the spectrum, is children. Leadership Columbus participants were advised that a growing number of children do not have access to adequate healthcare, as well as food, water, clothing, shelter, and safety. All of these are contributing to a growing worldwide problem where desperate people do desperate things.

The eleventh factor identified was global travel—the ability to transport communicable diseases around the world within a matter of hours. The twelfth factor was medical mutations—the super diseases, viruses, and bacteria becoming immune to the advances in medicine. Four forms of bacterial infection that could then be contracted in hospitals have no known antibacterial vaccination to either prevent or cure them. Of the twenty-five sexually transmitted diseases, five of them are incurable. There is no cure!

The graduates of Leadership Columbus were reminded that they were stepping into leadership roles in our community, state, nation, and world in which the issues of healthcare would be a major concern for the twenty-first century. Patients would soon have control, responsibility, and accountability for their healthcare and how it would be delivered.

A Revolution was coming!

Chapter Forty-Eight

The Healthcare Solution

In November of 1998, after three years of research and conversations with members of Congress, the author presented a proposal to members of Congress to amend the VEBA guidelines contained in the Employee Retirement Income Security Act of 1974. The minor amendment would make a major difference in the access to affordable healthcare. It was requested that Congress drop the restrictions in the current VEBA guidelines limiting participants "to the same line of business" in the same geographical area. Instead, allow employees in any size business—large, mid, small, and even self-employed persons—to participate in a community healthcare cooperative.

In March 2000 that proposal was presented by the author to SHRM (Society for Human Resource Management) Legislative Committee and SHRM Compensation and Benefits Committee, requesting its formal endorsement of a patient-controlled healthcare system proposal for a community healthcare cooperative. In March 2001, the proposal was presented to the AFL-CIO, U.S. Chamber of Congress, and the National Association of Manufacturers.

On April 28, 2001, at a local meeting of healthcare providers, participants were informed by the author of the new era in healthcare. The presentation was entitled "The Metamorphosis of Medicine." Participants were told of a new era in healthcare, best described by two words: "participant-directed." Participants were informed of customer-driven healthcare, consumer-driven healthcare, patient-controlled healthcare, and participant-directed healthcare. They were advised that managed care, as we know it, would be a thing of the past. The implications for providers would be a dramatic focus on customer service, because patients would decide which coverage, co-insurance, which physicians, specialists, and hospital they would go to and the treatment they would receive.

Another phrase that was mentioned to the group was "defined contributions." Employers would make defined contributions on behalf of their employees. This would restore the patient-doctor relationship, changing focus of that relationship from one of whoever provides the cheapest service to the one who provides the *best* service. This new delivery system would actually reduce paperwork and the amount of time physicians and staff spend negotiating for reimbursement. It would increase reimbursement so that providers are paid immediately by patients or promptly by third-party payors. Physicians and clinics would be the biggest winners.

The doctors were also encouraged by the hope of reduced hassles and greater freedom to provide good healthcare. There would be more use of team approaches to keeping people well and healthy. There would be an increasing focus on satisfying patients and relatives, the customer versus the payors and regulators. More important, physicians and hospitals would be paid but would also be sharing more risk.

Physicians were also introduced to preferred provider networks versus preferred provider organizations. A preferred provider network is a network of providers recommended by other providers, employers, patients, relatives, and payors.

A Revolution was coming!

CHAPTER FORTY-NINE

THE NEW HEALTHCARE PARADIGM

On October 10, 2001, the author went way out on a limb in an address to nearly three hundred civic leaders in a program entitled "The New Healthcare Paradigm." The participants were introduced to the phrases *participant-directed* healthcare and *defined-contribution* healthcare. They were told that a major paradigm shift from a plan-driven healthcare system to a participant-directed healthcare system would come in two to five years. Moreover, they were introduced to participant-directed, consumer-driven, and defined-contribution health plans. These phrases became common language in less than a year.

What drove this transition were more than twenty factors in three major categories that began with the letter "C." The first "C" was Courts—the actual and the threat of litigation. The second "C" was Cost. In the year 2001, the estimated costs in healthcare were projected at an 11 percent increase. The estimate for 2002 was 14 percent and for 2003 was 22 percent. The third "C" was Consumers. Access to the Internet, advertising, frustrations with the current systems, consumerism, aging population, entitlement mentality, and unhealthy lifestyles were driving healthcare into a new paradigm.

The audience was informed that efforts were already underway to change the way healthcare is delivered from a plan-driven healthcare system to a participant-directed healthcare system.

A Revolution was coming!

CHAPTER FIFTY

❧

BREAKING NEWS

Before October 10, 2001, I had no confirmation that the revolution had begun. Within weeks, however, confirmation appeared in print. In a special bonus section of *Time* magazine entitled "Your Business" (October 2001, p. 15), Daniel Isenberg published an article, "Stitch up an HMO." It was the tagline that was the most compelling. He wrote, "Workers may soon design and pay more for their health plans."

The article continued: "Bob Stevens knew something drastic had to be done. His company health insurance costs were soaring, up about 15 percent a year. At the same time his employees were becoming increasingly frustrated by the lack of alternatives to the restrictive managed care coverage he was buying—and Stevens runs a hospital.

"So last fall, Stevens, the CEO of Ridgeview Medical Center, a $110 million-a-year hospital and network of clinics in suburban Minneapolis opted for an experimental course of treatment. He offered his eight hundred full-time doctors, nurses, administrators, and other personnel the choice of a new scheme called 'a defined contribution' health plan, courtesy of a local start-up known as Definity Health. Unlike a traditional, narrowly defined set of health benefits, this plan lets

213

employees spend a portion of their allocated health dollars, usually around $1,000 to $2,000 per year, as they see fit. They can spend it on the deductible of a basic indemnity policy, or opt for alternative medicine. If they don't use up their allocation before the end of the year, they can roll it over to the next.

"At best, Stevens guessed, perhaps an adventurous 10-15 percent of the workers would take the leap. In the end though, more than 75 percent signed up. The results, said Stevens, is that 'we're creating savvy, healthcare consumers, who are really thinking about their money.' "

The article went on to say, "Some bosses are starting to think their employees might be the best weapon in the war against healthcare inflation. Much as 401k savings plans have supplemented old-fashioned, guaranteed pensions, such consumer-driven health plans aim to shift the responsibility and risk of employer health insurance to the rank and file employee."

The article quoted other people addressing the shift in thinking, such as Lee Newcomer. "'We've taught people that when they put down a $10 bill and an HMO card, they are entitled to everything,' says Newcomer, a managed care veteran and new Chief Medical Officer at benefits start-up VIVIUS."

There are several other start-ups involved in the defined contribution healthcare delivery systems including Lumenos, HealthMarket, HealthAllies, MyHealthBank, and perhaps most significant of all, Wellpoint out of California and Aetna, which just created its plan called HealthFund. Already, 5 percent of the U.S. businesses, including Medtronic, Narvartis, and Textron are testing some sort of defined contribution health plans. An additional 20 percent think it's likely that they will offer it in the next five years.

Isenberg goes on to suggest that there are several values to defined contribution plans. "Companies can—by paying a fixed amount each year instead of a percentage of ever-rising premiums—better predict and control the price of healthcare."

Providers will be more interested in these plans because "many of the most onerous restrictions of managed care, from pre-certifications and referrals to utilization review, are eliminated." And says Steve Wiggins founder of Oxford Healthplans and CEO of HealthMarket, "Eventually, the better doctors will get paid more." Providers will be paid instantaneously by HealthBank, which has partnered with Blue Cross Blue Shield to focus on small employers in the Northwest. He hopes eventually to offer consumers a debit card to have their visits to the doctor automatically paid out of their accounts.

The Revolution has begun!

᪻

CHAPTER FIFTY-ONE

CONFIRMED BY *THE WALL STREET JOURNAL*

On December 10, 2001, this revolution was given national status. An article in *The Wall Street Journal* entitled "Employers Expect Healthcare Costs to Rise 13 Percent in 2002" announced that companies were now offering their employees "defined contribution plans in which employees manage their own healthcare dollars."

The article, written by Barbara Martinez, staff reporter for *The Wall Street Journal* says, "The picture for health insurance costs keeps getting uglier for employers and consumers alike. Employers expect their healthcare costs to rise nearly 13 percent next year [2002], with some companies expecting to be hit with increases of 20 percent or more, according to a survey to be released today by human resource consulting firm, William M. Mercer, Inc."

She continues, "According to recent government projections, healthcare spending in the U.S. is expected to double over the next decade to $2.6 trillion, with U.S. businesses picking up a significant portion of the tab."

In response to costs, according to the survey, 40 percent of large employers said they were requiring employees to pay a higher percentage of the total cost next year by raising deductibles and co-pays. Already, the median in-network deductible for preferred provider plans has reached $500; for out-of-network deductibles $1,000-2,000 are not unusual.

Blaine Boss, a Mercer principal, expects double-digit healthcare inflation at least for the next four years. Certainly, there is the need, according to Martinez, to provide employees with more information about healthcare costs. But how can this be done? That's where defined contribution health plans come into play. According to the Mercer survey, 29 percent of employers with more than 20,000 workers said that they would somewhat or very likely adopt such an approach within the next two years.

The Revolution has begun!

❧

Chapter Fifty-Two

Recognized by *Psychotherapy Finances*

The cover story from *Psychotherapy Finances*, December 2001, was entitled "Are We Heading for a Self-Pay World?" According to this lead article, "The ground is shifting, as a growing number of employers are considering a dramatic change, downloading healthcare decisions and costs to their employees." The writer quotes the William M. Mercer survey, indicating that healthcare cost premiums rose 11.2 percent in 2001, and would go to 12.7 percent in 2002. Workers were paying substantially more in deductibles, doubling to $500 or $1000, with doctor visits costing $30 instead of the old $10 and $20 and patients even in HMO plans being required to pay $850 for a hospital admission instead of the previous $100. The article continued, "Defined contribution health plans are taking off" and related how major insurance companies like Humana, Cigna, United Health, and Wellpoint are jumping into the defined-contribution market with both feet.

Psychotherapy writers indicated that this could be as dramatic as the managed care revolution was as employers "end their role as primary financiers of healthcare. They are literally taking the insurance out of health insurance and introducing a world where healthcare consumers write the checks for their own healthcare."

The Revolution has begun!

CHAPTER FIFTY-THREE

BUSINESSES CONSIDER CUTS IN HEALTHCARE

On December 18, 2001, *The Wall Street Journal* carried another article entitled "Small Businesses Consider Cuts in Healthcare Costs." They, too, cite the William M. Mercer survey indicating a special alarm that smaller companies have already begun to shift an increasing amount of healthcare costs to workers by increasing insurance deductibles. What's more, "Mercer found that 13 percent of smaller companies and 6 percent of larger ones are considering an end to company-sponsored coverage. Those firms are considering instead paying workers more money and let them buy their own coverage."

The Revolution has begun!

❧

CHAPTER FIFTY-FOUR

H.R. NEWS ISSUES A WARNING

In the January 2002 issue of *H.R. News*, a news magazine for the Society of Human Resource Management, data from a recent Watson Wyatt survey was presented. "Fifty-six percent of employers plan to raise the employee contributions by as much as or more than their expected cost increases. Also, more than 70 percent of employers are considering reducing employee benefits or increasing employee co-payments next year." Employers expect health plan costs to rise 13.6 percent for active employees and 15.1 percent for pre-65 retirees. Prescription drug benefits are expected to jump a whopping 17 percent.

Clearly something drastic must be done—and done this year! Human Resource professionals are being asked for a solution.

The Revolution has begun!

CHAPTER FIFTY-FIVE

H.R. MAGAZINE COVER STORY

Perhaps the most significant signal of this revolution came in January 2002 when *H.R. Magazine* was mailed to over 170,000 human resource professionals across the country and around the world. It announced the coming of defined contribution health plans. The Society for Human Resource Management represents the human resource professionals and is the organization that has the greatest single influence on the practices of the profession. Compensation and benefits is one of the major areas of its focus and its monthly magazine. This focus certainly signals and addresses the major topics that are and will be facing human resource professionals.

The cover story of the January issue of *H.R. Magazine* was titled "Containing Growing Healthcare Costs." The tagline, written by Carol Herschman, is sure to reverberate throughout the employment world. It stated: "Defined contribution coverage is designed to cut costs by giving workers more control over their healthcare choices."

For the next four pages, this article introduced the human resource professionals to defined contribution healthcare plans. Herschman writes, "Few benefits are as difficult to manage as healthcare. Employers want to control skyrocketing premiums;

employees want more coverage at less cost, and H.R. gets caught in the middle juggling plan options and fielding complaints about health plan service.

"Lacking a magic wand to cure the ills of health coverage, many consultants are laying out what is called the defined contribution approach, which tries to marry consumer choice and cost savings. In defined contribution arrangements, participating employees have choices. For example, in 401k plans, employees choose from various investment options. In defined contribution health plans, employees choose the medical benefits that best suit their needs."

Herschman continues, "It's too soon to tell if the defined contribution approach will capture a substantial share of the insurance market. But for now, at least, an increasing number of employers are giving it a try."

She cites Radnor Holdings Corporation, a Pennsylvania-based manufacturer of styrofoam cups, Charter Communications, Inc., out of St. Louis, and Novartis Corporation, an international company. She also lists the providers—Aetna, Humana, Wellpoint, Blue Cross Blue Shield, Definity Health, Lumenos, and MyHealthBank. She writes, "Driving the defined contribution trend are rising medical costs, a backlash against managed care, and a growing perception that one size doesn't fit all when it comes to health benefits.

"Many employees are frustrated with managed care's strict rules and quality of care. Employers worry about getting sued by employees with gripes against managed care companies and about complying with ever-changing laws and regulations."

Tom Miller, CEO of Definity Health, a defined contribution insurer in St. Louis Park, Minnesota, says, "Employers are saying 'I can't do the same old, same old. I can't keep tweaking plan designs. I need a whole new approach.'"

Herschman claims that workers are now more diverse than ever, and their lifestyles may not be satisfied if the employer has only one plan. Employers also want out, at least in part, to avoid the expense and hassle of administering health insurance benefits. But they also want to treat their employees well by offering health coverage. Employers are hoping that defined contribution care will achieve both ends.

Thus, the Revolution has begun!

⅋

Chapter Fifty-Six

Where Are the Benefit Managers?

If the revolution is on, why haven't we heard about it? An intriguing article appeared in *Business and Health: State of Healthcare in America, 2001* issue, released in April 2001! It was the lead story written by Shelly Reese, entitled "Defined Contribution: The Undefined Concept." This excerpt perhaps says it all: "a new method for financing employee health benefits is said by many to be the hope of the future. But lack of understanding and a heavy dose of employer paternalism have kept the discussion theoretical. Defined contribution health plans may have consultants' tongues wagging, but they have employers' heads spinning. While pundits champion the healthcare financing method as a vehicle for controlling employer costs, benefit managers agree on the concept with yawning ambivalence."

According to a recent survey by *Business and Health* and Milliman and Robertson, the responses really show a lot of caution and paternalism in employer thinking. But even more than that, it shows how fearful employers are of change and the unknown. Only about half of more than four hundred human resource managers and benefit coordinators from medium-sized and large companies have even heard of a defined contribution healthcare plan. Less than one-third have a basic understanding of the plans.

Given the attention that consultants and industry publications have devoted to defined contributions, Clark Seifer, a consulting actuary in Milliman and Robertson's Milwaukee office says, "The lack of awareness is dumbfounding." He goes on to say, "These are not small employers. They are large companies with benefits specialists. You have to wonder where these people have been." Seifer points out, "The low level of understanding is particularly surprising given the fact that 401k plans provide a fairly analogous model for how defined contribution plans can work. Employers are not only unaware of defined contribution health plans, they are also uninterested." Those who responded who do understand defined contributions say they learned about it from industry and professional publications, benefit consultants, conferences, and trade shows. Notably absent from the list of informants, it should be pointed out, are other employers. Only two of nearly four hundred respondents say they learned about defined contributions from another employer.

According to Reese, there are a number of biases that have to be overcome. Employees prefer to have their employer choose their healthcare benefits. Employers lack confidence in the workers' ability to make informed healthcare choices. Employers are also hesitant to give up control of this area. Most employers think their employees are satisfied with their current plans. Another, of course, is that employers and employees are unaware of defined contribution health plans. They are also unclear of the taxation issues associated with these plans. And if employers make healthcare plans portable, it might decrease employee loyalty.

Reese presents the five factors that would influence employers' willingness to implement a defined contribution plan.

1. Greater predictability of costs.
2. Greater control over healthcare costs.
3. Lower administrative costs to the employer.
4. Increased sense of personal responsibility for health among employees.
5. Protection from liability suits.

Fortunately the results from the *Business and Health/* Milliman and Roberson survey indicates that the affect of defined contribution plans on employee loyalty would be by and large minimal—56 percent said that it would not affect employee loyalty and only 19 percent said it would decrease loyalty, while 13 percent said it would actually increase loyalty to their companies. Reese says that movement to defined contribution will really depend on a third force beyond the consultants' sphere of influence—leadership. The decision to adopt defined contribution is less a benefit manager's strategy for cost control than a chief executive's vision for employee empowerment.

Seifer says, "You need someone with a vision of what responsibilities they expect the employees to take and I think that decision is made at a relatively high level. They don't have to understand the details. They need to endorse the philosophy. And according to the survey, the likelihood of implementing a defined contribution plan if health benefits costs continue to increase, 50 percent said likely, 20 percent said highly likely, while 30 percent said not likely. So while the revolution has begun, it actually may be led by the leadership of companies rather than by benefit managers."

The Revolution has begun!

cb

HARVARD BUSINESS SCHOOL GETS ON BOARD

Regina Herzlinger, professor, Harvard Business School, champions defined contributions as the future of healthcare. In an article that appeared in *Business and Health*, 2001 (p.11), she says, "It will be an answer to rampant premium inflations, while insuring employees have coverage." Consumers will have the ability to choose the type of coverage that best suits their individual needs. It puts consumers in the driver's seat, which would have an added bonus for employers, relieving them of liability that might accompany patients' rights legislation. "In the long run, consumer-driven healthcare would likely result in a more rational, people-friendly delivery system." Perhaps most of all, according to this article, "cost may be the decisive factor."

Paul Dusseault, president of The Ad Group, a Eugene, Oregon-based advertising agency, recently switched to a defined contribution approach. For Dusseault, the time arrived last year when his HMO sought a 36 percent increase on top of a 47 percent hike the previous year. That sent Dusseault shopping. "I'd had it," he says. "The costs are rising far too fast. I can't kick my fees up 47 percent one year and 36 percent the next. I'd lose my customers." Fortunately or unfortunately, there are thousands of companies just like The Ad Group.

The Revolution has begun!

Chapter Fifty-Eight

The Kaiser Family Foundation Releases Findings

The Kaiser Family Foundation and the Health Research and Educational Trust released a survey in 2001 (*Business and Health*, 2001, p.13) that describes the most compelling factor behind the healthcare revolution. In 1998 the average premium rate increase was 12 percent. With the advent of HMOs, POSs, and PPOs, by 1993, it had dropped to an average of 8.5 percent and in 1996, down to less than 1 percent (0.8). But by 1999 the average cost of premiums had risen to 4.8 percent, one year later in 2000 it went to 8.3, by 2001 it had gone to 11 percent, and 2002 it was at 13.7 percent.

Ironically, health insurance leads the inflation pack. While the overall inflation in 1988 was 4.4 percent, healthcare inflation was 12 percent. In 1993 overall inflation was 3.2 percent; healthcare inflation was 8.5 percent. By 1999 the overall inflation was 2.1 percent, but healthcare had jumped to 4.8 percent. One year later in 2000, while overall inflation was 3.0 percent, healthcare had gone to 8.3 percent. General inflation has remained around 3 percent and healthcare is increasing nearly 15 percent every year.

Something must be done. Patients and providers, employers and their families all must share financial risk in healthcare decisions. Employees must be rewarded financially for staying healthy. Defined contribution healthcare plans such as medical spending accounts, healthcare saving accounts, and best of all, community healthcare cooperatives with HSAs accomplish these objectives.

The Revolution has begun!

ℭ

WAYNE B. ANTHONY,

M. DIV., MBA, CEAP, SPHR

SENIOR PROFESSIONAL IN HUMAN RESOURCES (SPHR)
CERTIFIED EMPLOYEE ASSISTANCE PROFESSIONAL (CEAP)

Wayne received a Bachelor of Arts degree in Psychology from Asbury College in 1971 and a Master of Divinity from Emory University in 1974. He completed a Masters of Business Administration from the University of Georgia in 1985 with an emphasis in Strategic Planning and Human Resource Management. In January 1997, Wayne completed graduate training in financial planning from Colorado's College of Financial Planning and is currently a Professional Financial Planner.

After eight years in corporate management with RJR Nabisco, Wayne returned to his hometown of Columbus, Georgia, in 1987 to direct the Financial Counseling Program and the Employee Assistance Program of a large mental health complex (Bradley Center/Pastoral Institute).

He is currently Director of The Business Resource Center, which provides employee assistance services, financial counseling services, management training and development services, and organizational planning and development services to more than 130 organizations throughout the United States.

In 1998, Wayne helped organize and then served four years as the Director of the Center for Servant Leadership, an initiative by area organizations and institutions to develop the attitude and skills of servant leadership within young people, managers, professionals and community leaders.

On January 1, 2000 Wayne helped launch House of Heroes, a joint initiative by local representatives of the Congress of the United States, the U.S. Chamber of Commerce, the Society for Human Resource Management, the Department of Defense, the Department of Veteran Affairs and Hands On/City Cares of America. House of Heroes honors elderly and disabled military and public safety veterans and/or their spouses by providing repairs and improvements to their homes.

For the last twenty-five years, Wayne has been involved in healthcare issues. He spent eight years (1979-1987) with R.J.R. Nabisco as a purchaser of healthcare. From 1987 to the present, he has been involved in the healthcare arena with purchasers, providers, payors, legislators, patients and relatives. In 1996, he was selected to serve as Georgia State Legislative Chair for the Georgia Society of Human Resource Management (SHRM) and in 2000 was invited to serve as a member of the National Legislative Committee of SHRM where he has focused on healthcare legislation.

Wayne is an ordained United Methodist minister having served appointments for thirty-four years. For the last fourteen years, he has been on special appointment to Asbury UMC, a multiethnic church located in a transitional neighborhood in South Columbus.

Wayne is also an elected official in Columbus. He serves as one of two citywide members of the City Council. As such, he represents all the people of Georgia's second largest city.

Wayne is married to Frances Sue Brown of Columbus. Frances Sue holds a Master of Science Degree in Community Counseling from Georgia State University and is a Licensed Professional Counselor at Columbus Psychological Associates. They have three adult children.

Wayne can be contacted at:
2022-15th Avenue
Columbus, GA 31901
Or email wanthony@pilink.org